AF010434

How to access your on-line resources

Kaplan Financial students will have a MyKaplan account and these extra resources will be available to you online. You do not need to register again, as this process was completed when you enrolled. If you are having problems accessing online materials, please ask your course administrator.

If you are not studying with Kaplan and did not purchase your book via a Kaplan website, to unlock your extra online resources please go to www.en-gage.co.uk (even if you have set up an account and registered books previously). You will then need to enter the ISBN number (on the title page and back cover) and the unique pass key number contained in the scratch panel below to gain access.

You will also be required to enter additional information during this process to set up or confirm your account details.

If you purchased through Kaplan Flexible Learning or via the Kaplan Publishing website you will automatically receive an e-mail invitation to register your details and gain access to your content. If you do not receive the e-mail or book content, please contact Kaplan Publishing.

Your code and information

This code can only be used once for the registration of one book online. This registration and your online content will expire when the final sittings for the examinations covered by this book have taken place. Please allow one hour from the time you submit your book details for us to process your request.

Please scratch the film to access your unique code.

Please be aware that this code is case-sensitive and you will need to include the dashes within the passcode, but not when entering the ISBN.

Professional Examinations

Strategic Level

Subject P3

Risk Management

EXAM PRACTICE KIT

SUBJECT P3 : RISK MANAGEMENT

Published by: Kaplan Publishing UK

Unit 2 The Business Centre, Molly Millars Lane, Wokingham, Berkshire RG41 2QZ

Copyright © 2017 Kaplan Financial Limited. All rights reserved.

No part of this publication may be reproduced, stored in a retrieval system or transmitted in any form or by any means electronic, mechanical, photocopying, recording or otherwise without the prior written permission of the publisher.

Notice

The text in this material and any others made available by any Kaplan Group company does not amount to advice on a particular matter and should not be taken as such. No reliance should be placed on the content as the basis for any investment or other decision or in connection with any advice given to third parties. Please consult your appropriate professional adviser as necessary. Kaplan Publishing Limited and all other Kaplan group companies expressly disclaim all liability to any person in respect of any losses or other claims, whether direct, indirect, incidental, consequential or otherwise arising in relation to the use of such materials.

British Library Cataloguing in Publication Data

A catalogue record for this book is available from the British Library

ISBN: 978-1-78415-937-5

Printed and bound in Great Britain

CONTENTS

	Page
Index to questions and answers	P.4
Examination Techniques	P.5
Syllabus Guidance, Learning Objectives and Verbs	P.7
Approach to revision	P.11

Section

1	Objective test questions	1
2	Answers to Objective test questions	81

Quality and accuracy are of the utmost importance to us so if you spot an error in any of our products, please send an email to mykaplanreporting@kaplan.com with full details.

Our Quality Co-ordinator will work with our technical team to verify the error and take action to ensure it is corrected in future editions.

INDEX TO QUESTIONS AND ANSWERS

OBJECTIVE TEST QUESTIONS

Page number

		Question	Answer
1 – 45	Identification, classification and evaluation of risk	1	81
46 – 99	Responses to strategic risk	14	87
100 – 148	Internal controls to manage risk	33	96
149 – 203	Managing risks associated with cash flows	50	104
204 – 256	Managing risks associated with capital investment decisions	63	115

EXAM TECHNIQUES

COMPUTER-BASED ASSESSMENT

TEN GOLDEN RULES

1. Make sure you have completed the compulsory 15 minute tutorial before you start exam. This tutorial is available through the CIMA website. You cannot speak to the invigilator once you have started.

2. These exam practice kits give you plenty of exam style questions to practise so make sure you use them to fully prepare.

3. Attempt all questions, there is no negative marking.

4. Double check your answer before you put in the final answer although you can change your response as many times as you like.

5. On multiple choice questions (MCQs), there is only one correct answer.

6. Not all questions will be MCQs – you may have to fill in missing words or figures.

7. Identify the easy questions first and get some points on the board to build up your confidence.

8. Try and allow 15 minutes at the end to check your answers and make any corrections.

9. If you don't know the answer, flag the question and attempt it later. In your final review before the end of the exam try a process of elimination.

10. Work out your answer on the whiteboard provided first if it is easier for you. There is also an onscreen 'scratch pad' on which you can make notes. You are not allowed to take pens, pencils, rulers, pencil cases, phones, paper or notes.

SYLLABUS GUIDANCE, LEARNING OBJECTIVES AND VERBS

A AIMS OF THE SYLLABUS

The aims of the syllabus are

- to provide for the Institute, together with the practical experience requirements, an adequate basis for assuring society that those admitted to membership are competent to act as management accountants for entities, whether in manufacturing, commercial or service organisations, in the public or private sectors of the economy;
- to enable the Institute to examine whether prospective members have an adequate knowledge, understanding and mastery of the stated body of knowledge and skills;
- to complement the Institute's practical experience and skills development requirements.

B STUDY WEIGHTINGS

A percentage weighting is shown against each topic in the syllabus. This is intended as a guide to the proportion of study time each topic requires.

All component learning outcomes will be tested and one question may cover more than one component learning outcome.

The weightings do not specify the number of marks that will be allocated to topics in the examination.

C LEARNING OUTCOMES

Each topic within the syllabus contains a list of learning outcomes, which should be read in conjunction with the knowledge content for the syllabus. A learning outcome has two main purposes:

1. to define the skill or ability that a well-prepared candidate should be able to exhibit in the examination;
2. to demonstrate the approach likely to be taken by examiners in examination questions.

The learning outcomes are part of a hierarchy of learning objectives. The verbs used at the beginning of each learning outcome relate to a specific learning objective, e.g. Evaluate alternative approaches to budgeting.

The verb 'evaluate' indicates a high-level learning objective. As learning objectives are hierarchical, it is expected that at this level students will have knowledge of different budgeting systems and methodologies and be able to apply them.

A list of the learning objectives and the verbs that appear in the syllabus learning outcomes and examinations follows and these will help you to understand the depth and breadth required for a topic and the skill level the topic relates to.

SUBJECT P3 : RISK MANAGEMENT

	Learning objectives	Verbs used	Definition
1	**Knowledge**		
	What you are expected to know	List	Make a list of
		State	Express, fully or clearly, the details of/facts of
		Define	Give the exact meaning of
2	**Comprehension**		
	What you are expected to understand	Describe	Communicate the key features of
		Distinguish	Highlight the differences between
		Explain	Make clear or intelligible/State the meaning of
		Identify	Recognise, establish or select after consideration
		Illustrate	Use an example to describe or explain something
3	**Application**		
	How you are expected to apply your knowledge	Apply	To put to practical use
		Calculate/compute	To ascertain or reckon mathematically
		Demonstrate	To prove with certainty or to exhibit by practical means
		Prepare	To make or get ready for use
		Reconcile	To make or prove consistent/compatible
		Solve	Find an answer to
		Tabulate	Arrange in a table
4	**Analysis**		
	How you are expected to analyse the detail of what you have learned	Analyse	Examine in detail the structure of
		Categorise	Place into a defined class or division
		Compare and contrast	Show the similarities and/or differences between
		Construct	To build up or compile
		Discuss	To examine in detail by argument
		Interpret	To translate into intelligible or familiar terms
		Produce	To create or bring into existence
5	**Evaluation**		
	How you are expected to use your learning to evaluate, make decisions or recommendations	Advise	To counsel, inform or notify
		Evaluate	To appraise or assess the value of
		Recommend	To advise on a course of action
		Advise	To counsel, inform or notify

D OBJECTIVE TEST

The most common types of Objective Test questions are:

- multiple choice, where you have to choose the correct answer from a list of four possible answers. This could either be numbers or text.
- multiple choice with more choices and answers – for example, choosing two correct answers from a list of eight possible answers. This could either be numbers or text.
- single numeric entry, where you give your numeric answer e.g. profit is $10,000.
- multiple entry, where you give several numeric answers e.g. the charge for electricity is $2000 and the accrual is $200.
- true/false questions, where you state whether a statement is true or false e.g. external auditors report to the directors is FALSE.
- matching pairs of text e.g. the convention 'prudence' would be matched with the statement' inventories revalued at the lower of cost and net realisable value'.
- other types could be matching text with graphs and labelling graphs/diagrams.
- In this Exam Practice Kit we have used these types of questions.

Some further guidance from CIMA on number entry questions is as follows:

- For number entry questions, you do not need to include currency symbols or other characters or symbols such as the percentage sign, as these will have been completed for you. You may use the decimal point but must not use any other characters when entering an answer (except numbers) so, for example, $10,500.80 would be input as 10500.80
- When expressing a decimal, for example a probability or correlation coefficient, you should include the leading zero (i.e. you should input 0.5 not .5)
- Negative numbers should be input using the minus sign, for example –1000
- You will receive an error message if you try to enter a character or symbol that is not permitted (for example a '£' or '%' sign)
- A small range of answers will normally be accepted, taking into account sensible rounding

Guidance re CIMA On-Screen calculator:

As part of the computer based assessment software, candidates are now provided with a calculator, although they can also use a physical calculator. This calculator is on-screen and is available for the duration of the assessment. The calculator is accessed by clicking the calculator button in the top left hand corner of the screen at any time during the assessment.

All candidates must complete a 15 minute tutorial before the assessment begins and will have the opportunity to familiarise themselves with the calculator and practise using it.

Candidates may practise using the calculator by downloading and installing the practice exam at http://www.vue.com/athena/. The calculator can be accessed from the fourth sample question (of 12).

Please note that the practice exam and tutorial provided by Pearson VUE at http://www.vue.com/athena/ is not specific to CIMA and includes the full range of question types the Pearson VUE software supports, some of which CIMA does not currently use.

The Objective Tests are ninety minute computer-based assessments comprising 60 compulsory questions, with one or more parts. CIMA is continuously developing the question styles within the system and you are advised to try the online website demo at www.cimaglobal.com, to both gain familiarity with assessment software and examine the latest style of questions being used.

APPROACH TO REVISION

Stage 1: Assess areas of strengths and weaknesses

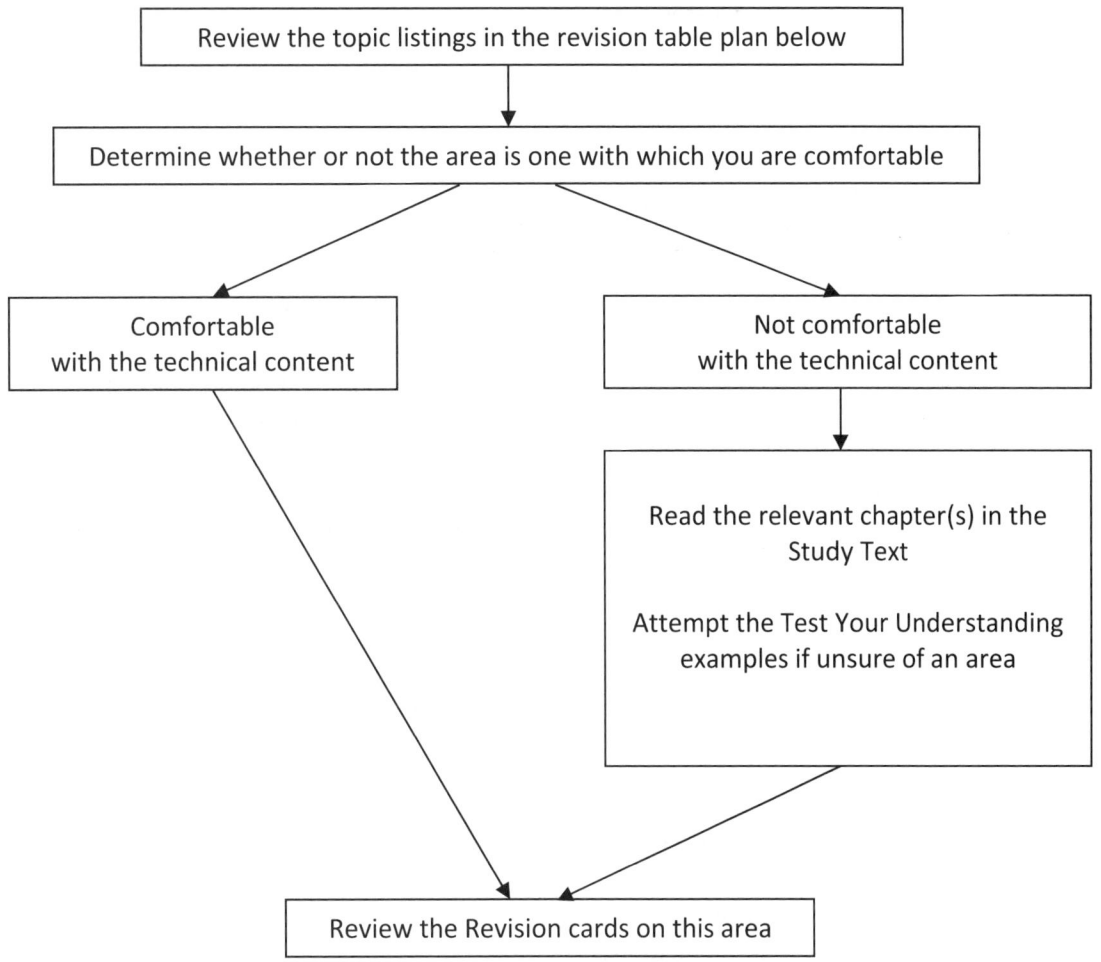

Stage 2: Question practice

Follow the order of revision of topics as recommended in the revision table plan below and attempt the questions in the order suggested.

Try to avoid referring to text books and notes and the model answer until you have completed your attempt.

Try to answer the question in the allotted time.

Review your attempt with the model answer and assess how much of the answer you achieved in the allocated exam time.

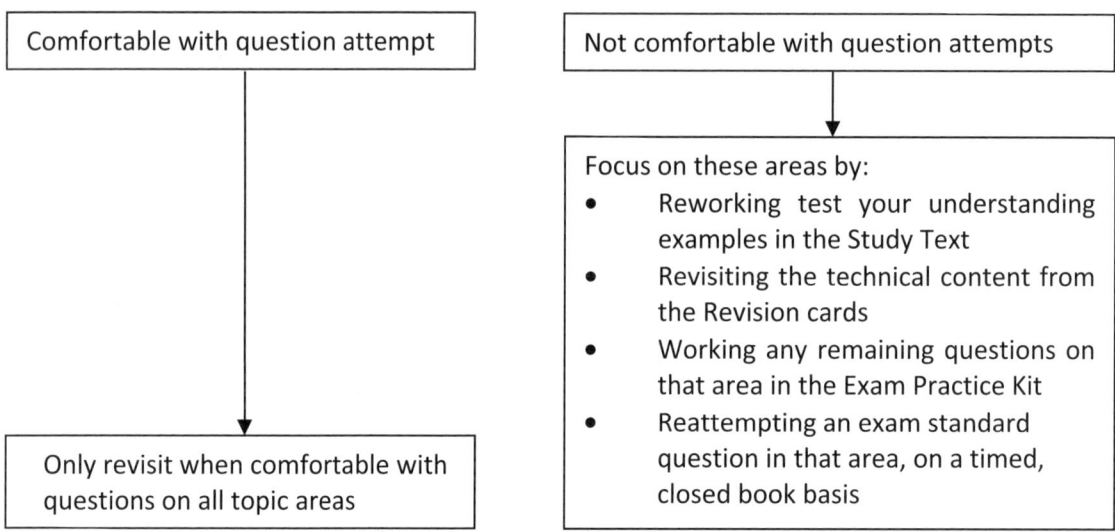

Stage 3: Final pre-exam revision

We recommend that you **attempt at least one ninety minute mock examination** containing a set of previously unseen exam standard questions.

It is important that you get a feel for the breadth of coverage of a real exam without advanced knowledge of the topic areas covered – just as you will expect to see on the real exam day.

Ideally a mock examination offered by your tuition provider should be sat in timed, closed book, real exam conditions.

P3
RISK MANAGEMENT

Syllabus overview

P3 shows how to identify, evaluate and manage various risks that could adversely affect the implementation of the organisation's strategy. It provides the competencies required to analyse, evaluate and apply the techniques, processes and internal control systems required to manage risk. This insight is then used to manage the risks associated with both cash flows and capital investment decisions – two important areas of organisational life for which the finance function is responsible.

Summary of syllabus

Weight	Syllabus topic
20%	A. Identification, classification and evaluation of risk
20%	B. Responses to strategic risk
20%	C. Internal controls to manage risk
20%	D. Managing risks associated with cash flows
20%	E. Managing risks associated with capital investment decisions

SUBJECT P3 : RISK MANAGEMENT

P3 – A. IDENTIFICATION, CLASSIFICATION AND EVALUATION OF RISK (20%)

Learning outcomes
On completion of their studies, students should be able to:

Lead	Component	Indicative syllabus content
1 evaluate the types of risk facing an organisation and recommend appropriate responses.	(a) identify the types of risk facing an organisation	<ul><li>Upside and downside risks arising from internal and external sources and from different managerial decisions.</li><li>Risks arising from international operations, such as cultural differences and differences between legal systems. **Note:** No specific real country will be tested.</li><li>Strategic and operational risks.</li></ul>
	(b) evaluate the organisation's ability to bear identified risks	<ul><li>Quantification of risk exposures (impact if an adverse event occurs) and their expected values, taking account of likelihood.</li><li>Risk map representation of risk exposures as a basis for reporting and analysing risks.</li></ul>
	(c) recommend responses to identified risks.	<ul><li>Enterprise Risk Management and its components.</li><li>Risk mitigation including TARA – transfer, avoid, reduce, accept.</li><li>Gross and net risks.</li><li>Assurance mapping and similar techniques for describing risks and their associated responses.</li></ul>
2 evaluate senior management's responsibility for the implementation of risk management strategies and internal controls.	(a) recommend techniques that will enable the board to discharge its responsibilities with respect to managing risks	<ul><li>The control environment.</li><li>Internal control.</li><li>Risk register.</li></ul>
	(b) advise the board on its responsibilities for reporting risks to shareholders and other stakeholders.	<ul><li>Risk reports and stakeholder responses.</li></ul>
3 evaluate the ethical impact of risk.	(a) evaluate ethical, social and environmental issues arising from risk management.	<ul><li>The identification of ethical dilemmas associated with risk management.</li><li>Reputational risks associated with social and environmental impacts.</li></ul>

P3 – B. RESPONSES TO STRATEGIC RISK (20%)

Learning outcomes
On completion of their studies, students should be able to:

Lead	Component	Indicative syllabus content
1 evaluate the tools and processes required for strategy implementation.	(a) recommend appropriate measures for the strategic control and direction of various types of organisations	• Business unit performance and appraisal, including transfer pricing and taxation, reward systems and incentives. • Non-financial measures and their interaction with financial measures. • Risks of performance measurement, including the Balanced Scorecard (BSC). • Lean systems. • Cost of quality. • Big Data as a strategic resource.
	(b) recommend solutions for the risks of dysfunctional behaviour arising from the associated models of performance measurement	• Dysfunctional behaviour associated with measures of control and direction.
	(c) advise managers of the risks in the development of strategies for information systems that support the organisation's strategic requirements.	• The purpose and contents of information systems strategies, and the need for strategy complementary to the corporate and individual business strategies.
2 evaluate ethical issues facing an organisation and its employees.	(a) evaluate the risks of unethical behaviour.	• Ethical issues identified in the CIMA Code of Ethics for Professional Accountants. • Application of the CIMA Code of Ethics for Professional Accountants. • The board's responsibilities for the management of stakeholders' interests.
3 evaluate the risks associated with corporate governance.	(a) evaluate the risks associated with poor governance structures.	• The separation of the roles of CEO and chairman. • The role of non-executive directors. • The roles of audit committee, remuneration committee, risk committee and nominations committee. • Directors' remuneration. • The agency implications of salaries, bonuses, performance-related pay, executive share options and benefits in kind.

SUBJECT P3: RISK MANAGEMENT

P3 – C. INTERNAL CONTROLS TO MANAGE RISK (20%)

Learning outcomes
On completion of their studies, students should be able to:

Lead	Component	Indicative syllabus content
1 evaluate control systems for organisational activities and resources.	(a) evaluate the appropriateness of control systems for the management of an organisation.	<ul><li>Application of control systems and related theory to the design of management accounting control systems and information systems in general.</li><li>Control systems within functional areas of a business including HR, sales, purchases, treasury, distribution, IT.</li><li>Identification of appropriate responsibility and control centres within the organisation.</li><li>Performance target setting.</li><li>Performance appraisal and feedback.</li><li>Cost of quality applied to the management accounting function and 'getting things right first time'.</li><li>Responses to risks in control systems for management.</li></ul>
2 evaluate risk management strategies and internal controls.	(a) evaluate the essential features of internal control systems for identifying, assessing and managing risks.	<ul><li>Minimising the risk of fraud: fraud policy statements, effective recruitment policies and good internal controls, such as approval procedures and separation of functions.</li><li>The risk manager role as distinct from that of internal auditor.</li><li>Purposes of internal control: the achievement of an entity's objectives, effectiveness and efficiency of operations.</li><li>Identifying and evaluating control weaknesses.</li><li>Identifying and evaluating compliance failures.</li><li>Operational features of internal control systems, including embedding such systems in a company's operations, responsiveness to evolving risks and timely reporting to management.</li></ul>

Learning outcomes
On completion of their studies, students should be able to:

Lead	Component	Indicative syllabus content
		• The pervasive nature of internal control and the need for employee training. • Costs and benefits of maintaining the internal control system. • Disaster recovery.
3 evaluate the purposes and process of audit in the context of internal control systems.	(a) evaluate the effective planning and management of internal audit and internal audit investigations.	• Forms of internal audit: compliance audit, fraud investigation, value for money audit/management audit, social and environmental audit. • Operation of internal audit, the assessment of audit risk and the process of analytical review, including different types of benchmarking, their use and limitations. • Effective internal audit: independence, staffing and resourcing, organisational remit. • The preparation and interpretation of the internal audit report.

SUBJECT P3: RISK MANAGEMENT

P3 – D. MANAGING RISKS ASSOCIATED WITH CASH FLOWS (20%)

Learning outcomes
On completion of their studies, students should be able to:

Lead	Component	Indicative syllabus content
1 evaluate financial risks facing an organisation.	(a) evaluate financial risks facing an organisation.	• Sources of financial risk associated with international operations. • Transaction, translation, economic and political risk. • Quantification of risk exposures, their sensitivities to changes in external conditions and their expected values. • Exposure to interest rate risks.
2 evaluate alternative risk management tools.	(a) advise on the effects of economic factors that affect future cash flows from international operations	• Exchange rate theory and the impact of differential inflation rates on forecast exchange rates. • Theory and forecasting of exchange rates (e.g. interest rate parity, purchasing power parity and the Fisher effect). • Value at risk.
	(b) evaluate appropriate methods for the identification and management of financial risks associated with international operations	• Minimising political risk. • Responses to economic transaction and translation risks. • Operation and features of the more common instruments for managing interest rate risk: swaps, forward rate agreements, futures and options. • Techniques for combining options in order to achieve a specific risk profile: caps, collars and floors. • Internal hedging techniques.
	(c) evaluate appropriate methods for the identification and management of financial risks associated with debt finance.	• Operation and features of the more common instruments for managing currency risk: swaps, forward contracts, money market hedges, futures and options. **Note:** The Black Scholes option pricing model will not be tested numerically. However, an understanding of the variables which will influence the value of an option will be assumed.

P3 – E. MANAGING RISKS ASSOCIATED WITH CAPITAL INVESTMENT DECISIONS (20%)

Learning outcomes
On completion of their studies, students should be able to:

Lead	Component	Indicative syllabus content
1 evaluate the risks arising from changes in the environment for capital investment appraisal.	(a) evaluate investment projects	<ul><li>Cost of capital and risk.</li><li>Recognising risk using the certainty equivalent method (when given a risk free rate and certainty equivalent values).</li><li>Adjusted present value. **Note:** The two step method may be tested for debt introduced permanently and debt in place for the duration of the project.</li></ul>
	(b) evaluate conflicts that may arise from capital investment decisions	<ul><li>Managing conflicts between different stakeholder groups (profit maximisation versus wealth maximisation).</li><li>Managing conflicts arising from performance indicators.</li></ul>
	(c) evaluate the outcomes of projects post implementation and post completion.	<ul><li>Monitoring the implementation of plans.</li><li>Post completion audit.</li></ul>

TABLES

Information concerning formulae and tables will be provided via the CIMA website, www.cimaglobal.com, and your MyKaplan login.

Section 1

OBJECTIVE TEST QUESTIONS

IDENTIFICATION, CLASSIFICATION AND EVALUATION OF RISK

A1: TYPES OF RISK

1 Which one of the following sentences best describes risk?

    A   The exposure to the adverse consequences of dangerous environments

    B   The expected impact of uncertain future events on objectives

    C   The chance of being caught doing something unethical

    D   The impact of the exposure to the adverse consequences of uncertain future events

2 Risk management is the process of reducing the adverse consequences either by reducing the _____ of an event or its _____.

What are the two missing words?

    A   Understanding and impact

    B   Likelihood and potential

    C   Understanding and potential

    D   Likelihood and impact

3 Risk appetite is determined by

    A   Risk attitude and risk awareness

    B   Risk attitude and risk capacity

    C   Risk strategy and risk awareness

    D   Risk attitude and residual risk

4 The four strategies in TARA for managing risk do NOT include which one of the following?

    A   Transference

    B   Approval

    C   Avoidance

    D   Acceptance

SUBJECT P3 : RISK MANAGEMENT

5   Risks can be categorised as either 'pure', 'speculative' or 'upside'. Drag and drop the following risks into the correct category.

	Pure risks	Speculative risks
The risk that a fire may destroy company assets		
The risk that a customer goes out of business		
The risk that a foreign exchange rate may change		
The risk relating to the level of future profits		
The risk that a capital investment may not yield the predicted IRR		
The risk that a virus is introduced to a computer application		

6   There are six steps in CIMA's risk management cycle. Identify the correct sequence of steps, by entering step numbers below.

Development of risk response strategy	
Implement strategy and allocate responsibilities	
Review and refine process and do it again	
Identify risk areas	
Implementation and monitoring of controls	
Understand and assess scale of risk	

7   Match each of the following risks to the appropriate risk category.

Risk category
Business risks
Economic risks
Environmental risks
Financial risks

Risk
Inflation rate rises
Exchange rate changes
Failure of a new product
Rate of climate change increases

8   Match each of the following risks to the appropriate risk category.

Risk category
Business risks
Economic risks
Corporate reputation risks
Political risks

Risk
CEO convicted of insider dealing
Disposable income levels fall
Nationalisation of industry
Raw material prices rise

9   Match each of the following risks to the appropriate risk category.

Risk category
Political risks
Legal risks
Regulatory risks
Compliance risks

Risk
Government increases rate of Corporation Tax
Company prosecuted for breach of the Data Protection Act
Change of Government
Customer sues company for negligence

OBJECTIVE TEST QUESTIONS : **SECTION 1**

10 X is a food manufacturer. X uses genetically modified (GM) ingredients in some of its products. A change in public opinion regarding GM foods represents which of the following types of risk? (One only)

A   Business risk

B   Economic risk

C   Reputation risk

D   Environmental risk

11 AA plc is a multinational company, retailing household electrical appliances. The finance director is concerned about the lack of risk management as at the present time AA plc only look at financial risk.

Select THREE of the following risk categories that would also be relevant for AA plc to assess:

A   Gearing

B   Product risk

C   Reputation risk

D   Risk response

E   Technological risk

F   Monitoring Risk

12 Viva plc is a large casino company, operating all over the world. Each casino is a multi-million pound construction project. Viva plc's current policy is to finance expansion using high debt levels.

Which THREE of the following risks would you identify as critical for Viva to assess?

A   Financial risk

B   Project risk

C   Foreign Exchange rate risk

D   Production risk

E   Health and safety risk

F   commodity price risk

SUBJECT P3 : RISK MANAGEMENT

13 OKJ is currently undertaking a risk analysis.

   Which TWO of the following factors are the most important risk issues facing OKJ?

   A   OKJ's home country has recently elected a new government. It is not yet clear if they will introduce new legislation to increase minimum wages. This would have a major impact on OKJ's profitability.

   B   After a recent accident in one of its factories, OKJ was convicted of breaching relevant health and safety legislation. Based on similar recent cases brought in the industry, OKJ expects to be fined around 7% of its turnover. OKJ has insurance in place that will cover this fine.

   C   OKJ uses platinum as a key component within some of its products. The price of metals varies significantly on world markets and tends to rise sharply in times of recession. The directors are concerned that its products may become unprofitable if platinum prices rise more than 20% from their current levels, but is uncertain about whether this would happen – even if a recession does occur.

   D   OKJ is uncertain about whether it can retain its CEO in the long term. It has had a number of CEO's over the last five years – each of them staying very different lengths of time in their roles. Fortunately, OKJ has an experienced Board of Directors and the change in CEOs has had little impact on the business in the past.

14 **One of the first steps in developing a risk management strategy is to determine the risk capacity, attitude and appetite of the organisation. Match the definitions with the terms below:**

Term	Definition
risk capacity	'the overall approach to risk'
risk attitude	'the amount of risk that the organisation is willing to accept in the pursuit of value added'
risk appetite	'the amount of risk that the organisation is able to bear'

15 **The Board of X is discussing risk. The first item for discussion is the organisation's 'risk appetite'. Which of the following factors determine the risk appetite of an organisation?**
   Select all that apply.

   A   The background of the board

   B   The number of directors

   C   The reputation of X

   D   The nature of the product or service of X

   E   Customer expectations

16 **The identification of risk is an important stage in developing a risk management strategy. Approaches to identifying risk are categorised as internal or external, and proactive or reactive.**

   The use of SWOT and PEST(EL) analysis are both examples of which approach?

   A   internal proactive

   B   internal reactive

   C   external proactive

   D   external reactive

17 'Be A Sport Ltd' is a medium-sized event organiser and is considering the following four possible strategies and how best to manage the risks involved:

1   A race event Be A Sport Ltd has organised for next week is an outdoors 5k run. However if it rains it is unlikely to attract enough competitors to make any profit. The management have decided to still hold the event.

2   Be A Sport Ltd has just taken out a large insurance contract to ensure they are covered if any competitor seeks damages for injuries caused in one of their races.

3   One of the employees at Be A Sport Ltd has had an innovative idea to hold a waterfall jumping event where competitors compete to jump from the highest possible place along a sheer cliff edge into the North Sea. After considering the idea the Be A Sport Ltd management have rejected it as it is too dangerous.

4   As part of the organisation of the huge annual showcase event Be A Sport Ltd hold, they have conducted a large and extensive risk assessment process and put into place all the internal controls they believe to be necessary.

Which strategy best fits the following four risk management methods?

A   Transfer

B   Accept

C   Reduce

D   Avoid

18 X is a company involved in oil exploration and extraction. Following a risk review, X has identified that earthquakes occur in its exploration areas once every five years, on average. The average cost of work to resume oil production, following an earthquake, is estimated to be US$ 30million.

Calculate the value of the risk of earthquakes, in US$, to the nearest million.

19 X is a financial institution, lending to consumers for the purchase of consumer durables. X currently has a total of £120 million lent to customers, and currently has $200,000 loans outstanding to customers. The management accountant of X has calculated that the likelihood of a customer defaulting on a loan is 2%.

What is the 'credit risk exposure' of X, on its consumer lending? Express your answer in £, rounded to the nearest million.

20 D, a finance manager, has been asked to forecast the sales for next year. The standard calculation with the organisation is to account for various probable outcomes using expected values. D has been given the following information by the Sales Manager

Forecast sales for next year	Probability of occurrence
£200,000	10%
£250,000	40%
£300,000	30%
£350,000	20%

Calculate which ONE of the following is the EXPECTED value of sales for next year?

A   £200,000

B   £260,000

C   £280,000

D   £240,000

21 Party Ltd is a successful family-run business retailing party ware from a small shop in the UK. The younger members of the business wish to open another larger shop in a neighbouring town and to expand into e-business, selling across the country via the Internet. However, the Managing Director, founder and mother of the younger family members has resisted all change and says that the business is doing fine without any change, so there is no reason to do anything.

Which ONE of the following Risk attitudes can you see being displayed by the Managing Director?

A   Risk seeking

B   Risk cautious

C   Risk averse

D   Risk taker

22 'Risk mapping' is a technique that is commonly used to show risks on a matrix. Which TWO variables form the 'axes' or 'dimensions' of a risk map?

A   Source

B   Category

C   Probability

D   Department

E   Impact

23 The sudden death of the CEO of a small marketing consultancy would best fit which category in a risk map?

A   Low probability; low impact

B   Low probability; high impact

C   High probability; low impact

D   High probability; high impact

24 X is a large retailer, employing over 20,000 sales staff. The retail industry has a reputation for a high level of staff turnover. The resignation of a member of the sales staff would best fit which category in a risk map?

A   Low probability; low impact

B   Low probability; high impact

C   High probability; low impact

D   High probability; high impact

OBJECTIVE TEST QUESTIONS : **SECTION 1**

25 **The 'TARA' mnemonic is often used to categorise risk management methods. Which one of the following represents the methods in the TARA mnemonic?**

- A   Transfer; Assure; Remove; Accept
- B   Transfer; Accept; Reduce; Adapt
- C   Transfer; Avoid; Reduce; Accept
- D   Transfer; Accept; Remove; Adapt

26 **'Net risk' (also known as 'residual risk') is calculated by multiplying probability and impact _____ any action is taken to mitigate the risk.**

Which word correctly completes the sentence above?

- A   Before
- B   After

27 C Company has recently expanded and now trades in two different countries. Country A is a developed nation with a sophisticated legal system and democratic government.

Country B is a democracy but has a history of corruption and fraud at the highest levels of government.

The board of C Co has noticed that in Country B costs of setting up new premises have been unusually high. On questioning the managers within Country B, the board has learned that 'additional payments' to officials must be made in order to obtain planning permission. In Country A, these kinds of payments would be illegal. Managers in both countries are paid bonuses according to the success of C Co's expansion plans.

The board has decided to prevent these additional payments from being made in the future in order to be able to establish the same ethical standards in both countries. Company C is pursuing an expansion strategy in both countries.

What are the possible risks arising from C Company preventing these payments in future?

Select all that apply.

- A   Further expansion in Country B will not occur.
- B   Expansion in Country A will slow.
- C   Staff turnover in Country B will increase.
- D   Overall performance of C Company will suffer.
- E   C Company's ethical reputation will suffer.

28 Q is a house builder operating in Country P where interest rates are at their lowest point for 20 years. The government of Country P has been encouraging the building of new houses due to a shortage, particularly of 'affordable housing'. Q has taken full advantage of government schemes to help the population purchase new housing and has invested in new machinery, taken on extra staff and begun to build on many of the sites held in its 'land bank'.

Government schemes of particular interest to Q include low interest rate government loans, government backed mortgages and the ability to purchase a share of a home, with the government owning the remaining amount on which rent would be paid according to market rates.

As part of Q's regular risk register review, the possibility of interest rate increases has been flagged.

What are the potential consequences for Q of an increase in interest rates?

A   Those customers who have purchased houses via government schemes may default on their loans.

B   Q may find demand for its new houses decreases.

C   Q's own costs may increase.

D   The government may withdraw their schemes leading to a drop in demand.

E   The cost of land will increase.

29 J is an organisation which provides veterinary services to large producers of meat and dairy produce in Country P. Lately J has found it difficult to recruit enough qualified veterinarians despite offering excellent terms and conditions. This is partly due to a shortage of newly qualified veterinarians in Country P where training has become very expensive.

J has also had problems sourcing some of the antibiotics and vaccinations it routinely sells to customers for their animals. There is a great deal of controversy surrounding medical intervention into meat and dairy produce and some of J's usual suppliers have had their production disrupted by violent protests. There are many other suppliers of these goods in other countries.

J offers a 24hr support service to its larger customers where it will attend any unexpected emergency or event and offer veterinary services. Recently J was sued by one customer who had used this service when hundreds of cows became suddenly ill on a weekend. Many of the cows died despite J's intervention. Uptake of this 24hr support service is very low since J's customers do not generally feel it is necessary and J is likely to settle the court case soon at great expense.

Directors have also noticed that equipment they issue to staff is getting lost or damaged far more lately and this is adding extra costs to the services they offer. J is unable to increase prices due to the competitive nature of the industry so keeping costs low is very important.

Which of the following would appear to be valid risk management techniques for J?

Select all that apply.

A   Transfer the risk of damaged or lost equipment to an insurance company.

B   Reduce the risk of not attracting staff by increasing pay offered significantly.

C   Accept the risk of being unable to source vaccinations and antibiotics.

D   Avoid the risk of further court cases by no longer offering the 24hr support service.

A2: SENIOR MANAGEMENT RESPONSIBILITY FOR RISK MANAGEMENT

30 F, an internal auditor working for ABC plc, a medium-sized building contractor firm, is concerned with the risk management process with ABC. F has investigated the process at each organisational level extensively and found that, although ABC do identify risks and then respond, the cognitive process involved in analysing the likelihood and impact for each identified risk is not being systematically conducted.

Distinguish which ONE of the following steps are missing from ABC's risk management process.

- A   Control activities
- B   Reporting
- C   Risk Assessment
- D   Compliance

31 The Committee of Sponsoring Organisations of the Treadway Commission (2003) have developed a three dimensional matrix Enterprise Risk management (ERM) framework

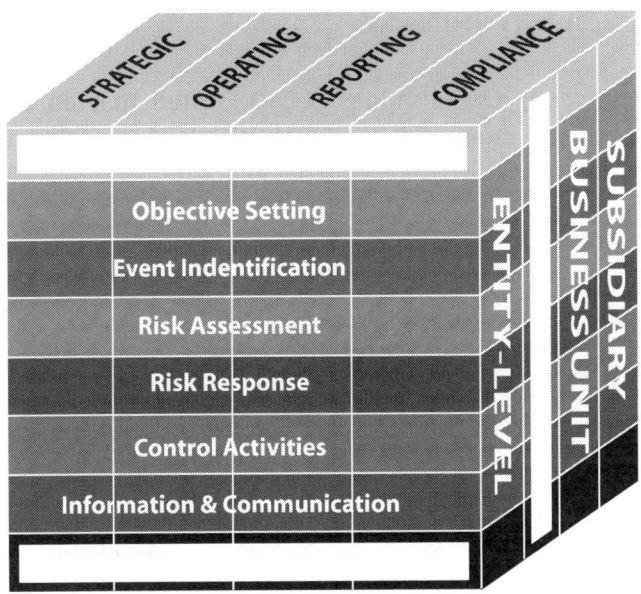

Which THREE are the missing elements of the ERM framework pictured above.

- A   Division
- B   Monitoring
- C   Internal environment
- D   PEST
- E   core competencies
- F   Analysis

SUBJECT P3 : RISK MANAGEMENT

32   The Committee of Sponsoring Organisations (COSO) outlined six key principles of Enterprise Risk Management (ERM). Identify which of the following is/are included. Select all that apply.

   A   Consideration of risk management in the context of business strategy
   B   The creation of a risk aware culture
   C   Consideration of a narrow range of risks, mainly financial
   D   Risk management is the responsibility of the Risk Committee
   E   A comprehensive and holistic approach to risk management

33   X is planning to produce its first 'risk register'. Which of the following aspects of each risk should be included in such a document? Select all that apply.

   A   The probability or likelihood of the risk
   B   The name of the risk owner
   C   Actions to be taken to mitigate the risk
   D   The impact of the risk
   E   The level of residual risk associated with the risk

34   In 1992, the Committee of Sponsoring Organisations (COSO) stated that an effective internal control system consists of five integrated elements. Which of the following are elements of such a system, according to COSO? Select all that apply.

   A   Risk assessment
   B   A risk register
   C   An internal audit function
   D   A control environment
   E   Control activities

35   Health plc is a leading innovative pharmaceutical research and manufacturing company with interests across the globe. Yesterday a leading newspaper in a developing country exposed a serious and potentially deadly health risk to employees being exposed to harmful chemicals.

   Health plc has not yet reacted to the report and the management are in emergency meetings to decide on the best course of action. Within the meeting the newly appointed Finance Manager remarked on the lack of regard for employees by local managers and a culture of carelessness and neglect.

   Which ONE element of the COSO framework for Internal controls is the Finance Manager discussing?

   A   Control environment
   B   Risk assessment
   C   Control activities
   D   Monitoring

36 According to the Financial Reporting Council (FRC) in its version of the Turnbull Report, which of the following is ultimately responsible for a company's system of internal controls?

- A The Financial Controller
- B The Board of Directors
- C The Internal Audit function
- D Every employee

37 The influential in the UK Turnbull report (1992), stated there are three features of a sound internal control system

Which THREE of the following best describes those three features within the Turnbull report?

- A The principle of Internal control is embedded into the organisation.
- B The board of Director must resign if any internal control failure is found.
- C An organisations' internal control system must be able to respond to changing risks from within and outside the company.
- D An internal auditor must be appointed by every organisation.
- E The internal control system must include a robust and rigorous procedure for reporting.
- F The shareholders must be informed of all internal controls in place in the annual report.

38 X is a retailer of fruit and vegetables. X has recently acquired a number of farm businesses. This is an example of which type of integration?

- A Forward Vertical
- B Backward Vertical
- C Horizontal
- D Conglomerate

39 S is a large multinational organisation which operates in many different markets and manufactures many different products. It considers itself to be a conglomerate. The complexity of S's operations has made risk management very difficult in the past since each strategic business unit is so different.

The board of S has recently employed a team of external consultants and asked them to produce and maintain a risk register for S.

The consultants are working on the risk register, which is to be a document with a tabular format and various headings.

Which of the following headings could the board of S expect to see in the risk register produced for S? Select all that apply.

- A Risk Owner
- B Mitigation Actions
- C Overall Risk Ratings
- D Risk Appetite
- E Risk Capacity

SUBJECT P3 : RISK MANAGEMENT

A3: THE ETHICAL IMPACT OF RISK

40 **X is concerned about risks to its corporate reputation. Identify which of the following risks directly affect the reputation of X?** Select all that apply.

- A A key supplier of X is based in a 'low wage economy', and is known by X to employ staff as young as 8 years of age.
- B The packaging used by X is not recyclable, and contains small traces of a known toxin.
- C X delivers its products by road and air.
- D X pays staff at levels below the average for its industry.
- E X does business with several non-democratic or repressive governments.

41 MLC is a clothing retailer who imports clothes from diverse suppliers worldwide. MLC has a very strong, well publicised corporate ethical code. The company accountant has just found out that one of MLC suppliers use child labour in the manufacture of their clothes and pay very low wages with cramped, dangerous conditions. This is in breach of contract conditions with that supplier.

What actions should MLC take in the light of this?

- A Place more orders with the supplier – it's cheap labour so the margins are good, which should keep the shareholders happy.
- B Leave things as they are and hope the information doesn't get out.
- C Continue trading with the supplier but investigate the claims quietly.
- D Cancel all contracts with the supplier and release a press statement stating how the company will always act quickly and decisively if unethical practices are suspected.

42 **The legal position of the whistleblower is covered within the Public Interest Disclosure Act 1998. Under that Act, 'malpractice' can take which of the following forms?** Select all that apply.

- A Criminal offences
- B Failure to comply with a legal obligation
- C Miscarriage of justice
- D Threats to health and safety
- E Damage to the environment

43 You are a management accountant working a UK listed chemical company. During the course of your duties, you become aware that the company is dumping waste illegally. You have raised this with your manager who has told you to ignore the issue.

Which of the following is NOT an appropriate course of action to take next?

- A Contacting CIMA's ethical helpline for advice
- B Reporting the company to the environment agency
- C Contacting a journalist at a national newspaper
- D Taking the matter to the Audit committee

OBJECTIVE TEST QUESTIONS : **SECTION 1**

44 Which THREE of the following are common arguments FOR organisations adopting a strong approach to corporate social responsibility (CSR)?

- A Increased profitability due to cost reductions
- B Faster strategic decision-making
- C Improved reputation with environmentally conscious customers
- D Ability to attract higher calibre staff
- E Reduced risk of government intervention in the future

45 HH is a fashion retailer, selling women's clothing in developed countries. HH's customers expect prices to be kept very low and since the market is so competitive, these customers can easily switch to HH's rivals if they do not like the styles or prices on offer in HH's chain of 300 shops.

HH sources garments from many different suppliers but recently the board has learnt that one of its main suppliers has been using child labour in the manufacture of HH's products. Child labour is not illegal in the developing country this supplier operates in and is culturally acceptable there.

HH is aware that child labour is not acceptable in the developed countries where it sells its products. Continued use of the supplier in question is likely to lead to international media coverage and this could subsequently lead to significant damage to HH's reputation.

However, HH has committed to purchase hundreds of new designs from the supplier and if they are no longer able to deal with them, in the short term inventory will be low and customers will be lost.

The board of B have decided to ignore the use of child labour at the supplier for now and deal with media coverage and response as and when it occurs. A plan to introduce minimum standards for suppliers will be unveiled when media coverage occurs and should help manage any controversy.

Which of the following are likely risks resulting from this course of action? Select all that apply.

- A Risk that the company's clothing sales fall if media coverage occurs sooner than expected.
- B Risk that HH cannot source an alternative supplier if necessary.
- C Risk that HH's costs increase.
- D Risk that the company's decision to wait and see becomes public and the company is seen as unethical.

SUBJECT P3 : RISK MANAGEMENT

RESPONSES TO STRATEGIC RISK

B1: TOOLS AND PROCESSES FOR STRATEGY IMPLEMENTATION

46 XYZ is a medium sized pharmaceutical company. XC has at present a decentralised structure with five separate autonomous divisions divided by clinical need, for example. Division A focuses on cancer research, Division B on tropical diseases, etc. Expertise is highly valued in the wider industry, where headhunting is common. Transfers of expertise and drugs between divisions are widespread.

Which THREE of the following are the most important potential issues that XYZ may encounter due to the divisional structure?

- A Autonomy
- B Lack of goal congruence
- C Growth
- D Maintaining a record of movement of goods and services between divisions
- E De-motivation
- F Devising fair and motivational divisional performance measures

47 The Finance Director of Huron plc – a large, complex organisation – is considering changing its system for transfer pricing.

Identify which THREE of the following issues the FD should consider, when considering what criteria a good transfer pricing policy should meet?

- A It should provide motivation for divisional managers.
- B It should be cheap to run.
- C Transfer pricing policy doesn't matter as it is only moving resources between internal SBU's.
- D It should allow divisional autonomy and independence to be maintained.
- E It should allow divisional performance to be assessed objectively.

48 Division X of James Ltd is considering a project which will increase annual net profit after tax by £30,000, but will require average inventory levels to increase by £200,000. The current target return on investment is 13% and the imputed interest cost of capital is 12%.

In these circumstances would the performance evaluation system's return on investment (ROI) and residual income (RI) motivate the managers of division X to act in the interests of the company as a whole?

	ROI	RI
A	Yes	Yes
B	Yes	No
C	No	Yes
D	No	No

OBJECTIVE TEST QUESTIONS : SECTION 1

49 Nova plc is a large, decentralised organisation with 20 divisions. Divisional managers are currently assessed using divisional return on investment (ROI) set against a company-wide target of 15%. Unfortunately the Board have found a number of instances where divisional managers have made decisions that improve their ROI but have eroded shareholder value.

Which TWO of the following proposals will have the best chance of rectifying this situation?

- A Sack all divisional managers that are subsequently found to have eroded shareholder value as this should encourage the others to think more from a company perspective.
- B Set targets based on Economic Value Added (EVA^{TM}) rather than ROI.
- C Set targets based on Residual income (RI) and ROI.
- D Offer divisional managers share options as part of their remuneration package to ensure goal congruence.
- E Insist that all projects are assessed using NPV and set monthly targets based on cash flow rather than profit.

50 Division D of Erie Ltd is considering a project which will increase annual profit by $15,000, but will require average receivables levels to increase by $100,000. The company's target return on investment is 10%, and the imputed interest cost of capital is 9%. Division D currently earns a return on investment of 16%.

Would the return on investment (ROI) and Residual Income (RI) performance measures motivate the manager of Division D to act in the interest of Erie Ltd as a whole?

- A The ROI would motivate the manager to act in the interest of the company as a whole, but the RI would not.
- B The RI would motivate the manager to act in the interest of the company as a whole, but the ROI would not.
- C Both the ROI and the RI would motivate the manager to act in the interest of the company as a whole.
- D Neither the ROI nor the RI would motivate the manager to act in the interest of the company as a whole.

51 TM plc makes components which it sells internally to its subsidiary RM Ltd, as well as to its own external market. The external market price is $24.00 per unit, which yields a contribution of 40% of sales. For external sales, variable costs include $1.50 per unit for distribution costs, which are not incurred on internal sales.

TM plc has sufficient capacity to meet all of the internal and external sales. The objective is to maximise group profit.

At what unit price should the component be transferred to RM Ltd?

- A $1.50
- B $12.90
- C $14.40
- D $24.00

SUBJECT P3 : RISK MANAGEMENT

52 Muddy plc has two divisions, A and B, which manufacture bicycles.

Division A produces the bicycle frames, and Division B assembles the bicycles components onto the frame. There is an external market for both the frames and an external market for the final product.

Both divisions are profit centres. The transfer price for the frame Division A produces has been set at the long term average market price. The following data are available for each division for the Coyote model:

- Estimated selling price for final product £300
- Long term selling price for frame Division A £200
- Incremental costs for completion in Division B £150
- Incremental costs in Division A £120

The divisional management in B has made the following calculations:

- Selling price for final product £300
- Less: Transferred-in market costs £200
- Incremental costs for completion £150
- Contribution on final product £(50)

Which ONE of the following statements is TRUE for Muddy plc for the Coyote model?

A   If there are capacity constraints, then in order to maximise return, Division A should satisfy its external market first, then transfer to Division B.

B   Muddy plc should cease production of Coyote bicycles.

C   It doesn't matter what Division A charges Division B.

D   If there are capacity constraints, then in order to maximise return, Division A should transfer frames to Division B before looking to sell frames externally.

53 Which THREE of the following are drawbacks of using the Balanced Scorecard (BS) model?

A   The BS does not provide a single view of performance which can lead to confusion.

B   There is no clear link between the balanced scorecard and shareholder analysis.

C   The BS mainly focuses on short-term measures, leading to long-term problems.

D   The BS forces each division within an organisation to use identical indicators.

E   Measures within the BS can conflict with each other, leading to confusion.

54 Alpha and Beta are two divisions of a company. Alpha manufactures two products, X and Y. X is sold outside the company. Y is sold only to division Beta at a unit transfer price of £88. Unit costs for product Y are

	£
Direct materials	30
Direct labour	20
Variable overhead	20
Fixed overhead	10
	80

Division Beta has received an offer from another company to supply a substitute for Y for £76 per unit.

Assuming division Alpha is only operating at 80% of capacity, if Beta accepts the offer the effect on profits will be

	Division Alpha profit	Overall Company profit
A	Decrease	Decrease
B	Increase	Decrease
C	Decrease	Increase
D	Increase	Increase

55 Decentralized organizations can delegate authority and still maintain control and monitor managers' performance by designing appropriate management control system.

Which of the following responsibility centres would be evaluated similar to an independent business?

A   Profit centre

B   Revenue centre

C   Investment centre

D   Discretionary cost centre

56 Which of the following statements is (are) true regarding managerial decisions?

A   The design and use of management control systems affects how an individual makes and implements decisions.

B   Rational managers will always make decisions that are in the best interest of the organisation employing them.

A   Only A is true

B   Only B is true

C   Both A and B are true

D   Neither A nor B is true

SUBJECT P3 : RISK MANAGEMENT

57 Global Stores Inc ('GS') is a large multinational retailer famous for its low prices and high value for money. GS has subsidiaries in many different countries and tax jurisdictions and uses transfer pricing to manage its global tax liability. GS and other global companies are coming under increasing criticism in Country E for paying no corporation tax despite revenues exceeding $50 million. Questions have been asked in parliament and the Government of E is now considering changing its tax rules or even imposing a special super tax on prime offenders.

Identify the best response to the criticism:

A   Release a press statement highlighting the fact that GS is doing nothing illegal and, by saving tax, is creating benefits for its shareholders, staff and customers.

B   Ignore the criticism as most customers will be more interested in GS's lower prices than its record on taxation.

C   Make a large donation to a high profile charity in Country E, ensuring it receives maximum publicity as a result.

D   Open discussions with the tax authorities of Country E to negotiate a fairer system of transfer pricing where it pays tax in E without massively increasing global tax liabilities.

58 Having attended a recent conference on the benefits of Big Data, the Marketing Director of YFT plc, an online retailer, has increased the number of sources it uses to gather information about customers in order to target them with appropriate advertisements and offers. His main concern is that, with so many different sources, there is an increased risk of inaccuracies and hence poor targeting.

Which ONE aspect of Gartner's 4Vs model is the Director having difficulties with?

A   Veracity

B   Velocity

C   Volume

D   Variety

59 J is a senior manager at a hospital. Currently, eye surgeons perform an average of 3 operations per day and this has left the hospital with a sizeable waiting list for such operations. J wishes to raise this to 5 per day. While he is not offering surgeons a bonus for achieving this new level of performance, he is sure that, as it will benefit patients, they will happily accept the new targets.

J has announced the new targets to his surgeons, who were annoyed as J had not previously consulted them about this issue. Privately most surgeons have admitted that they could reach 4 operations per day if they hurried through more routine procedures.

Which ONE of the following problems is J most likely to face with the new targets?

A   Surgeons will see the targets as unachievable and thus become demotivated by them.

B   Surgeons will rush operations, leading to poorer outcomes for patients and damage to the hospital's reputation.

C   Surgeons will demand that they will only work towards the new targets if they receive bonuses.

D   Surgeons will ignore the targets and do as they have always done.

60 Five years ago, PJ chose to compete on the basis of differentiation and so created a set of performance measures for its employees based on high quality production processes. However, the market has now changed and PJ is aware that it needs to lower its cost base to compete with new rivals entering its market. PJ has attempted to change its key performance measures, but has met with significant resistance from staff.

According to Berry, Broadbent and Otley, which ONE of the following problems with performance management systems is PJ experiencing?

- A Gaming
- B Sub-optimisation
- C Ossification
- D Tunnel-vision

61 **Which THREE of the following are the most important pre-conditions for the successful implementation of Just-in-Time (JIT) systems?** Select all that apply.

- A Predictable demand
- B Flexible manufacturing systems
- C Price stability
- D Co-operation of suppliers
- E Small batch quantities

62 **The 'costs of quality' can be categorised under four headings. Match each cost with the appropriate category.**

Category
Prevention costs
Appraisal costs
Internal failure costs
External failure costs

Cost
Re-working rejected output
Customer returns
Quality circles
Inspection of finished goods

63 Bee Town has a tourist information centre which relies on a local government grant to operate. The grant is about to be renegotiated and the manager of the centre expect the local government to try and reduce the amount they award.

The centre mainly offers advice and information to tourists over the phone or in person. They also act as an agency selling tickets to local attractions. The centre stocks leaflets and information produced and supplied by the local attractions themselves.

It is difficult to measure the performance of the centre since it does not directly generate revenue. However, the manager believes it significantly increases the amounts tourists spend in Bee Town's economy.

He wishes to use a balanced scorecard approach to demonstrate the performance of the information centre to the government at the grant negotiations.

SUBJECT P3 : RISK MANAGEMENT

Which of the following are suitable measures to include in the balanced scorecard? Select all that apply.

- A Percentage of visitors who rate the overall Bee Town visitor experience as good or excellent.
- B Percentage of stakeholders who consider the tourist information service to be good or excellent.
- C Number of tickets to local attractions sold by the centre.
- D Number of queries dealt with each day.
- E Average time taken to deal with each tourist query.

64 B is a large professional firm of financial advisors which offers bespoke project management services to clients. These services are generally one off in nature and each manager within B is assessed on the successful completion of client projects.

Each project is different and on occasion it is necessary to bring in external expertise to ensure the client gets the specialised service they request. B has an approved list of external consultants which managers can use if they feel it is required.

Over the last quarter, the use of external experts has increased by over 40%. The profit margin is falling as a result of this and the senior management are concerned that unnecessary costs are being incurred to enable managers to sign off projects quickly.

Which of the following actions might be appropriate to improve this situation? Select all that apply.

- A Revision of the management reward structure to include use of in house expertise.
- B Negotiation of cheaper outsource rates with external experts.
- C Abolition of the approved list of external consultants.
- D Introduction of a policy whereby senior management must approve all use of external consultants.
- E Monitoring of each project managers use of external experts.

65 Fred is the manager of a toy shop. The shop is part of a large chain of similar retail outlets all selling the company's own brand toys. Fred believes there is a market locally for beach toys since his shop is located by the sea however these kinds of toys are not part of his employers' product range. Fred believes one of the reasons for the underperformance of his shop is the presence of a competitor in the town with a more extensive range of toys including beach toys.

Fred's employer gives him responsibility for staff, premises and all other aspects of the shops day to day running. All other decisions are made centrally. Fred receives a bonus based on the shop's performance. He has not received his bonus due to the poor performance of the shop for three consecutive years.

Which of the following performance measures are likely to demotivate Fred if his bonus is based on them? Select all that apply.

- A Revenue growth.
- B Growth in net profit.
- C Control of overheads.
- D Return on investment.
- E Staff turnover.
- F Customer satisfaction.

66 Goggle plc is a multi-national software company. They have a head office in London and further large offices on each continent. They employ over 20,000 staff. It is a modern company with forward-thinking directors who believe that if staff are happy Goggle will receive their best work.

Goggle has installed non-work areas and activities at each office to keep its staff happy. For example, each major office has a 'play area' where there is a gym, table tennis, pool tables, a small crazy golf course and the like, which staff may access at any time subject to performing their work duties.

The average cost of one play area has been around £1 million.

Which of the following are possible non-financial benefits at Goggle? Select all that apply.

- A Increased productivity
- B Increased efficiency
- C Increased expenditure
- D Increased staff satisfaction

67 LAP is an external training organisation. They teach trainee computer programmers' basic skills early in their career – usually in the first few weeks of gaining employment, and usually for the next three years of their careers. The trainees are awarded a Diploma by LAP which is highly prized and often ensures a well-paid job in the future.

Tutors at LAP work in one of 12 offices around the UK – all in large cities. LAP cannot employ enough tutors with the correct skills mainly due to the salary being offered – it is insufficient ($150 per day) compared to the salary which could be earned outside of LAP. (LAP tutors also receive a pension, holiday pay, travel expenses, etc.) Staff at LAP are utilised only 65% of the time but their skills vary and any one tutor cannot teach all courses.

LAP often employ freelancers to cover any gaps and pay them in excess of a full-time LAP employee. This is well-known amongst LAP staff, and the braver ones have left LAP to return on a freelance basis, increasing their earnings considerably (a fixed fee of $300 per day).

Where possible LAP move staff across offices to cover any courses that do not have a tutor. There is a recharge of $350 per day from one office to another.

Which of the following should LAP do to become more cost efficient? Select all that apply.

A   Employ more skilled full-time staff on a higher salary.

B   Offer current staff overtime.

C   Always use full-time staff from other offices before freelancers.

D   Only use freelancers.

68   J is a manufacturer in the Midlands. It makes several different types of components for installation in washing machines.

Mr F has recently been appointed to the board of J. His previous employer had just started a 'lean management' initiative whereby the company was to cut out any unnecessary activities and reduce waste. Mr F is now hoping to undertake the same initiative at J.

J operates five cost centres – cutting, moulding, installation, maintenance and the canteen. Each cost centre reports variances from the budget each month. Any variances are usually small due to the experienced and hardworking labour force, and the reliable suppliers, which J has dealt with for decades.

The employees at J are highly motivated and there is rarely any downtime due to them. Absence through illness is very low.

Due to the number of components J manufactures there is often significant quantities of inventory within the factory and the warehouse. J supplies, on an ad hoc basis, to three major washing machine manufacturers who constantly trade off J and its competitors on the basis of price and ability to supply at short notice.

Mr F has been studying the activities at J and has identified three possible lean 'improvements'.

Which THREE of the following actions should Mr F suggest to the board of J?

A   J should reduce the number of cost centres.

B   J should produce the variance report on a quarterly basis.

C   J should eliminate their labour utilisation report.

D   J should not perform an annual inventory count.

69   Managers need to choose information system to support business strategies. Classify the following descriptions using the types of system given:

Description	Type of system
These systems allow senior managers to make strategic level decisions.	Executive information
These systems handle large volumes of operational-level data, and support structured decision making.	Management information
These systems allow any user with basic training to make semi-structured or unstructured decisions.	Expert
	Transaction processing
	Decision support

70 Many organisations set up a 'steering committee' to oversee systems development. The purpose of a steering committee is to do which of the following? Select all that apply.

- A Manage projects
- B Develop new systems
- C Consider the competitive issues raised by IT
- D Plan for new systems
- E Ensure that systems projects achieve the goals of the organisation

71 When a new information system is being developed, or an existing system revised, such development should be carefully controlled.

Which of the following are examples of system development controls? Select all that apply.

- A System testing
- B Training
- C Formal authorisation of system design
- D System documentation
- E Passwords

72 X is a multi-site organisation, formed by the recent merger of five organisations. Each site currently uses a different information system for the recording and processing of raw material inventory. It is planned to replace these systems with one new system that will be common to every site.

Which of the following system changeover methods may be used? Select all that apply.

- A Direct
- B Parallel
- C Pilot
- D Phased

73 Direct changeover is assumed to be the highest risk alternative available.

Which TWO of the following controls can mitigate the risk of system failure during direct changeover

- A Testing
- B Training
- C System documentation
- D Data backup
- E Check digits

74 Piccalilli Plc is a kitchenware retailer in the UK. They stock an unrivalled selection of kitchen utensils from essentials like dish cloths and draining racks to unusual ideas like a glass sided toaster.

The management are currently reviewing their performance appraisal procedures and have decided to implement some new measures.

Which of the following would be appropriate measures for Piccalilli Plc? Select all that apply.

- A   Percentage of the workforce attending a training course each year
- B   Revenue market share
- C   Number of customer complaints
- D   Year on year percentage revenue change
- E   Percentage of revenue generated from new products
- F   Number of new products in store
- G   Mystery shopper feedback scores

B2: ETHICAL ISSUES FACING AN ORGANISATION

75 The CIMA Code of Ethics contains five fundamental principles of professional ethics for management accountants. **Which of the following are fundamental principles, according to the Code?** Select all that apply.

- A   Confidentiality
- B   Honesty
- C   Objectivity
- D   Respect
- E   Integrity

76 Which THREE of the following are valid reasons for disclosing commercially sensitive information to a third party which would NOT breach the ethical principle of confidentiality?

- A   It is required due to a professional, ethical dilemma
- B   It is permitted by law and authorised by the client
- C   It is required by law
- D   Failure to disclose could materially disadvantage the third party
- E   There is a professional duty or right to disclose the information

77 John is a CIMA Member in Practice, and advises a range of individual clients and organisations. John has been asked by a client to write to one of the client's customers, threatening to report them to the tax authorities if they do not pay a debt due to John's client.

To do this would be in breach of which fundamental ethical principle (according to CIMA's Code of Ethics)?

A   integrity

B   objectivity

C   professional competence and due care

D   confidentiality

E   professional behaviour

78 Graham is a CIMA Member in Practice, and advises a range of individual clients and organisations. Graham has been asked, by his sister, to prepare her tax return. Graham's sister has offered to share any reduction in tax, compared to what she paid last year.

To do this would be in breach of which fundamental ethical principle (according to CIMA's Code of Ethics)?

A   integrity

B   objectivity

C   professional competence and due care

D   confidentiality

E   professional behaviour

79 Peter is a CIMA Member in Practice, and advises a range of individual clients and organisations. Peter has not carried out any Continuing Professional Development (CPD) activity for five years.

This is in breach of which fundamental ethical principle (according to CIMA's Code of Ethics)?

A   integrity

B   objectivity

C   professional competence and due care

D   confidentiality

E   professional behaviour

80 Gregor is a CIMA Member in Practice, and advises a range of individual clients and organisations. Gregor has been asked, by a prospective new client, to divulge details of another client's business activities.

To do this would be in breach of which fundamental ethical principle (according to CIMA's Code of Ethics)?

A integrity

B objectivity

C professional competence and due care

D confidentiality

E professional behaviour

81 CIMA's Code of Ethics recommends a four-step process to resolve any ethical conflict. **Identify the correct sequence for those steps.**

Refuse to remain associated with the conflict	
Check the facts	
Escalate externally	
Escalate internally	

82 John is a CIMA member, working as Financial Controller of a listed public company. John has shares in the company, and knows that the share price depends to some extent on the reported profits. John is responsible for producing the published accounts of the company.

According to CIMA's Code of Ethics, which TYPE of ethical threat does this represent?

A self interest

B self review

C advocacy

D intimidation

E familiarity

83 Gemma is a CIMA member, working as Financial Controller of a listed public company.

The company is in the process of applying for additional loan finance. Gemma has been asked to write to the company's bank, providing a forecast of future cash flows which she knows to be very optimistic.

According to CIMA's Code of Ethics, which TYPE of ethical threat does this represent?

A self interest

B self review

C advocacy

D intimidation

E familiarity

84 Stephanie has worked in the finance department of Alpha for 5 years and has been promoted to work alongside the management accountant. Stephanie is currently working towards a CIMA qualification.

The CIMA qualified management accountant of Alpha, has told Stephanie that he works closely with department heads to produce their annual budgets. He is happy to allow significant 'slack' to be built in to these budgets to make them easier to achieve since, in his view, this makes Alpha a much more relaxed place to work.

Following this conversation, Stephanie overheard the management accountant agreeing to alter budgeted production figures to make them easier to achieve in return for tickets to a major football game. When she questioned her boss, he told her no harm was done since the budgeted figures are subjective anyway.

Which of the following ethical principles is the management accountant in breach of?

Select all that apply.

A   Integrity.

B   Objectivity.

C   Professional competence and due care.

D   Confidentiality.

E   Professional Behaviour.

85 TC is a travel company. Its head office is in Germany but it operates throughout Europe. It is a multi-million dollar business with thousands of employees at head office, in high-street branches throughout Europe, and within the hotels it sends customers to.

TC has been in the world news recently due to a tragic event which occurred six years ago at one of the hotels it contracts with. Two children died in their hotel room due to a faulty boiler giving off poisonous carbon monoxide fumes while they slept.

The parents of the children have spent the past six years fighting for compensation from TC. The court case heard how TC contracted for rooms in the hotel. Part of the contract stated that the rooms should be 'safe' for their customers. The hotel manager signed the agreement but made no effort to check each room for its safety.

The parent's contract was with TC. TC's contract was with the hotel. The court case has now been decided and TC has been awarded $3 million in compensation. The hotel had broken its contract by not making the rooms safe. The parents were awarded nothing by the court since their contract was with TC, who had done nothing contractually wrong.

TC's Board has since decided to give the parents $350,000 as a gesture of goodwill. TC's actions have been criticised in the national press and on international television. TV coverage is showing parents packing carbon monoxide detectors in their suitcases prior to travelling to Europe. Interviews with parents have covered their disgust at TC's actions. No apology has ever been given by TC.

TC's share price has fallen by 10% over the past week.

This morning TC's Board announced their profits for the year and their CEO is to be awarded an $11 million bonus.

SUBJECT P3 : RISK MANAGEMENT

Which THREE of the following courses of action are most appropriate for TC?

A   TC should issue an apology to the parents.

B   TC should award the full $3 million to the parents.

C   TC should abide by the ruling of the court case.

D   TC should investigate every hotel room for safety.

E   TC should be pleased that the court case has raised the awareness of the TC brand.

86 CHB is a CIMA qualified accountant. She decided to leave her job as a management accountant at XYZ plc to start her own business. As a dog lover she opened a dog grooming salon in a town near to her home. She rented premises, just off the high street and near the local park, from the local council. The rent was advertised as $4,500 per annum but, due to the dilapidated state of the premises, she managed to negotiate a discount and paid only $350 per month. The council required one months' rent to be paid up front in lieu of a bond.

CHB employed two members of staff – one a qualified groomer, and one as a trainee groomer. The trainee groomer attended college on day per week, leaving the groomer to work alone that day. CHB managed the bookings, the bank account, wages, advertising and inventory.

The business quickly established itself and word spread in the local area that the service provided was good. Many customers returned every six to eight weeks, happy with the service. However, the local area didn't appear to have sufficient dogs to maximise capacity, so CHB had to terminate the trainee's employment contract (within her three month probation period). The disgruntled trainee did not receive the news of losing her job well and decided to take revenge by discrediting the business. Having copied the client details of some of the salons best customers she telephoned them at home and told them of terrible things that were done to their beloved pets while at the salon. These events were not true.

By the end of the first nine months it became apparent that the business would do well for one individual .i.e. the groomer (whose wages were fixed) but there was insufficient profit left over for CHB to take a salary. CHB decided to sell the business, which the groomer was more than happy to buy. The agreed purchase price was $5,000. This was paid immediately.

The rental agreement between CHB and the council continued until the year end. CHB still had to pretend that she was the business owner or she would be in breach of contract – one of the contract terms was that there was to be no sub-letting. On two occasions when the council telephoned CHB's home telephone number she pretended that she still ran the business. The groomer agreed with the charade.

CHB continued to pay the rent to the council each month until the contract end, the groomer having paid CHB first.

CHB paid the rent by debit card over the telephone. One month, towards the end of the rental contract, the council misallocated the rent received by them and allocated it in error to their rates department. The grooming business was rates exempt so the rates department returned the $350 to CHB.

At the end of the year, after receiving the bond back, CHB immediately closed the grooming business bank account and changed her telephone number. The council have not been in touch about the 'missing' months' rent yet.

Which THREE of the following ethical principles has CHB and her staff NOT met?

A   Integrity

B   Objectivity

C   Confidentiality

D   Professional behaviour

E   Professional competence and due care

B3: CORPORATE GOVERNANCE

87   Which one of the following is NOT a benefit of corporate governance?

A   Improved access to capital markets

B   Stimulation of performance

C   Enhanced marketability of goods and services

D   Prevention of fraudulent claims by contractors

88   The 'agency problem' refers to which of the following situations?

A   Shareholders acting in their own short-term interests rather than the long-term interests of the company.

B   A vocal minority of shareholders expecting the directors to act as their agents and pay substantial dividends.

C   Companies reliant upon substantial government contracts such that they are effectively agents of the government.

D   The directors acting in their own interests rather than the shareholders' interests.

89   Which TWO of the following are functions of audit committees?

1   Planning the annual external audit.

2   Reviewing the effectiveness of internal financial controls.

3   Reviewing and monitoring the external auditor's independence.

4   Processing year end journal adjustments to the financial statements.

A   1 and 2

B   1 and 3

C   2 and 4

D   2 and 3

90 Which of the following is the main reason for the roles of the chairman and chief executive to be held by different people?

   A   To ensure that there is more than one person overseeing the organisation.

   B   To ensure decision making power is not concentrated in the hands of one individual.

   C   To ensure the CEO can manage staff whilst the chairman meets potential investors.

91 The UK Corporate Governance regime recommends that large listed companies should form an Audit Committee consisting of independent non-executive directors. The Audit Committee should be responsible for which of the following? Select all that apply.

   A   Carrying out internal audit activities

   B   Managing internal audit activities

   C   Recommending appointment, or removal of the company's external auditor

   D   Reviewing the company's system of internal financial controls

   E   Carrying out external audit activities

92 The UK Corporate Governance regime recommends that large listed companies should form a Remuneration Committee. The Remuneration Committee should be responsible for which of the following? Select all that apply.

   A   Setting the remuneration level of the Executive Directors

   B   Setting the remuneration level of the Chairman

   C   Recommending on the remuneration level of the Senior Managers

   D   Setting the remuneration level of the Non-Executive Directors

   E   Setting the remuneration level of the External Auditor

93 The remuneration committee of Ghee plc, a listed company, consists of 4 Directors with the HR Director chairing the committee. The other three members are NED's although only one of these has been assessed as independent by the nominations committee. The remuneration committee has responsibility for both executive and non-executive pay policy with these policies being put forward by approval at the AGM by shareholders.

   What actions should Ghee take to comply with best practice corporate governance? Select all that apply.

   A   HR Director should resign from Ghee

   B   HR director should resign from the chairman position of the remuneration committee

   C   Non-independent NED should resign from the remuneration committee

   D   Remuneration committee should not have responsibility for NED remuneration

   E   All NEDs on remuneration committee should be replaced

OBJECTIVE TEST QUESTIONS : SECTION 1

94 Monk plc, a listed entity, currently has a governance structure that consists of an Executive Chairman, who acts as both Chairman and CEO, together with 4 executive directors and 1 non-executive director. What would you recommend in order for Monk plc to comply with best practice corporate governance?

   A   Removing the non-executive director as he/she is unlikely to have much knowledge of the business due to a lack of day to day involvement.

   B   Creating a separate role for chairman and CEO to replace the current role of Executive Chairman, recruiting an independent person for the position of chairman and recruiting additional non-executive directors to create a more balanced board.

   C   Replacing the role of Executive Chairman with the post of CEO and recruiting additional non-executive directors to create a more balanced board.

95 Which of the following does NOT represent good corporate governance?

   A   Membership of the audit committee should include at least three non-executive directors.

   B   Ensuring that non-executive directors do not participate at board meetings.

   C   Segregation between the roles of chairman and chief executive officer.

   D   At least one member of the audit committee should have recent, relevant financial experience.

96 Which of the following remuneration package elements for Directors will best ensure goal congruence between the interests of shareholders and executive directors?

   A   Cash bonus paid to directors if the company achieves profit growth targets.

   B   Cash bonus paid if directors achieve a range of individual performance related targets linked to the balanced scorecard.

   C   Share option bonus scheme that is paid if the company achieves profit growth targets.

   D   Private Health insurance for directors and their immediate family.

97 YY is a large listed company which makes soft drinks. The company has just experienced a very volatile 3 year period. During this time, the additive used to sweeten YY's products was made illegal in many of its core markets. In addition, the CEO and chairman both resigned and the Finance Director was removed following a conviction for insider training.

The new CEO has a strong manufacturing background but no direct experience of the soft drinks industry. At the next board meeting he wishes to discuss the role of NED's in supporting him given this lack of expertise. In his opinion, the NED's main function is to ensure the strategies of YY are realistic and achievable.

The company has 4 NED's, 2 of whom held senior positions in the soft drinks industry before their retirement from full time work. All four NED's have been in post for over 5 years.

Which of the following roles should the CEO expect the NED's to carry out in order to support him? Select all that apply.

- A   The setting of new strategies for YY.
- B   The scrutiny of strategies already proposed by the board.
- C   The monitoring of strategies for excessive risk.
- D   The analysis of the external environment.
- E   The recruitment of a new Finance Director.

98 According to a recent analyst's report, F is the only company out of the 150 biggest in Geeland which still has a unified chief executive-chairman.

Over the last year, several key investors have expressed concern that this is the case and urged the board of F to consider splitting the roles. In their opinion, an independent chair of the board of directors would eliminate the structural conflict of interest caused by the chief executive being his own boss, and would clarify where the authority of the chief executive ends and responsibility of the board begins.

The board of F are however happy with the current situation and have no plans to change.

Which of the following are likely arguments to maintain a unified chairman and chief executive role at F? Select all that apply.

- A   The board has appointed a senior independent director with the authority to act as though he or she were the non-executive chairman when required.
- B   Chairing the board in a large institution is a heavy workload and the pressures and breadth of responsibility borne by the chief executive are now almost beyond the capacity of a single person.
- C   There are many examples of corporate failure where the roles of chief executive and chairman were split.
- D   A combined CEO and chairman role will command a much higher level of remuneration than a single role of CEO.
- E   A board led by an independent chair is more likely to identify and monitor areas of the company that are drifting from its mandate and to put into place corrective measures to get it back on track.

99 The board of Bax Miking Plc have recently decided to appoint some new members to the board. The marketing director has put his daughter forward. His daughter Z, who is 23, has just completed studying towards a financial qualification in her first full time job. He feels that she would be a great addition to the board and would be able to join both the audit committee, and the remuneration committee.

Which of the following statements are true? Select all that apply.

A   Z could be an independent non-executive director for Bax Miking Plc.

B   Z's financial expertise would make her an ideal candidate for the audit committee.

C   Z should not be on the audit committee.

D   It would not be good corporate governance to have Z on the remuneration committee.

E   Z is unlikely to have enough experience.

F   Z would need to have worked at Bax Miking for 5 years before she could become a director.

G   Z needs to have more qualifications before she would be able to work on the board at Max Biking Plc.

INTERNAL CONTROLS TO MANAGE RISK

C1: CONTROL SYSTEMS

100 Information system controls can be classified as either general, application, software or network controls.

Match the examples below to the appropriate category.

Category
General
Application
Software
Network

Example
Licenses
Check digits
Anti-virus software
Passwords

101 Information system controls can be classified as either general, application, software or network controls.

Match the examples below to the appropriate category.

Category
General
Application
Software
Network

Example
Firewalls
Training
Pre-numbered forms
Licenses

SUBJECT P3 : RISK MANAGEMENT

102 Information system controls can be classified as 'security controls' and 'integrity controls'. Drag and drop the following controls into the correct category.

	Security	Integrity
Locked doors		
Passwords		
Batch totals		
Reconciliation		
CCTV		
Check digits		
Authorisation of data entry		
Fire alarms		

103 The Data Protection Act contains eight 'data protection principles'. **Identify which of the following are data protection principles.** Select all that apply.

    A   Personal data shall be confirmed with the data subject.

    B   Personal data shall be accurate and kept up to date.

    C   A data subject is responsible for the security and protection of data.

    D   A data subject is entitled to access and to have data corrected or erased.

    E   Personal data shall be held and used only for specified purposes.

104 The Data Protection Act covers a wide range of information systems. **Identify which of the following are exempt from one or more of the principles of the Act.** Select all that apply.

    A   Bank records

    B   Manual records

    C   Medical records

    D   Payroll records

    E   Crime records

105 DF plc has identified a critical success factor (CSF) for its organisation:

'Having an excellent quality product.'

Which ONE of the following would be the most suitable key performance indicator for this CSF?

    A   Reduce the number of defects identified by quality control and customers by 15%.

    B   Reduce the average time taken to deal with complaints about quality by 10%.

    C   Increase quality by 50% over the next year.

    D   Increase the amount of quality training for production staff.

OBJECTIVE TEST QUESTIONS : SECTION 1

106 S is a recently qualified Management Accountant who has just started working at Bob Ltd, a small building firm based in the UK.

One of S's duties is to oversee the internal controls of the company. However S is not sure how far her remit extends, as she is unsure what is covered by the term 'internal controls'

Which ONE would best describe the broad term of internal controls

- A A financial restriction place on the company.
- B An activity, which has been ordered to be completed by the auditors of a company.
- C An activity, which is in place to control certain risks and to help an organisation achieve its objectives.
- D An activity the human resources department conducts to ensure all employees are doing their job correctly.

107 SSS plc is a supermarket based in the UK and another European country. SSS's internal auditor has identified the following risks and internal controls to reduce those risks

Reconcile the FOUR risks to the FOUR internal controls.

Internal Controls	
A	Prepare and reconcile budget to actual spend
B	Hedging techniques
C	Tight stock control systems
D	CCTV cameras in store

Risks	
1	The risk of overspending on a construction project
2	The risk of employees stealing products
3	The risk of obsolescence, due to items with a short period of consumption
4	The risk of exchange rate fluctuation between Stirling and the Euro.

108 Which TWO of the following are objectives of the controls in the revenue cycle?

1. Goods are only supplied to customers who pay promptly and in full
2. All purchases are made with reliable and competitively priced suppliers
3. Orders are despatched promptly and in full to the correct customer
4. Only genuine employees are paid

- A 1 and 2
- B 1 and 3
- C 2 and 3
- D 3 and 4

109 Which TWO of the following are objectives of the controls in the payroll cycle?

1. Expenditure is recorded accurately and related payables are recorded at an appropriate value.
2. All purchases and related payables are recorded.
3. Correct amounts owed are recorded and paid to the taxation authorities.
4. Employees are paid at the correct rate of pay.

SUBJECT P3 : RISK MANAGEMENT

- A 1 and 2
- B 1 and 3
- C 2 and 3
- D 3 and 4

110 Which TWO of the following controls in a purchase cycle could be implemented to reduce the risk of payment of goods not received?

1 Sequentially pre-numbered purchase requisitions and sequence check.

2 Matching of goods received note with purchase invoice.

3 Goods are inspected for condition and quantity and agreed to purchase order before acceptance.

4 Daily update of inventory system.

- A 1 and 2
- B 2 and 3
- C 2 and 4
- D 3 and 4

111 Which TWO of the following controls in the purchase cycle could be implemented to reduce the risk of procurement of unnecessary goods and services?

1 Centralised purchasing department.

2 Sequentially pre-numbered purchase requisitions and sequence check.

3 Orders can only be placed with suppliers from the approved suppliers list.

4 All purchase requisitions are signed as authorised by an appropriate manager.

- A 1 and 3
- B 1 and 4
- C 2 and 4
- D 3 and 4

112 X is a manufacturing company. It makes one product, the Y. The quality inspectors of X currently reject 3% of the finished Ys produced, as they are unfit for purpose. Which of the following controls should reduce the rejection rate? Select all that apply.

- A Increased training of quality inspectors
- B Increased training of production staff
- C Purchasing higher quality raw materials
- D Better finished goods inventory handling procedures
- E Employing more quality inspectors

OBJECTIVE TEST QUESTIONS : **SECTION 1**

113 X is a retailer. It currently suffers significant losses due to theft by staff and customers. **Which of the following controls should reduce the number of thefts?** Select all that apply.

  A   Employing more security guards

  B   Improving staff selection procedures

  C   Reducing inventory levels

  D   Installing CCTV systems in stores

  E   Making suppliers responsible for the cost of thefts

114 In Country A, a person over the age of 17 can drive a car on public roads only if they have passed a one hour long practical driving test with an official examiner. This test involves the candidate demonstrating several driving skills but the route and the skills chosen are at the examiner's discretion. There are 350 test centres across Country A with each employing at least 3 examiners. Examiners do not work in more than one centre.

It has been reported in the media that in some centres, fewer than 30% of candidates are passing the practical exam, whereas the pass rate is as high as 80% in others. As a result, there has been much criticism of the lack of standardisation in tests and centres with low pass rates are seeing a reduction in demand whist those with higher rates have long waiting lists.

Country A's government officials have issued a statement in response to these reports saying that, although they have the utmost faith in driving test standards in the whole of Country A, they will be implementing further standardisation measures across all centres.

Which of the following ideas for standardisation may help to reassure learner drivers the test is the same wherever it is taken? Select all that apply.

  A   Increase in standard examiner training periods.

  B   Rotation of examiners around centres.

  C   Longer tests of 90 minutes duration.

  D   Increase of driving age to 18.

  E   Creation of a more detailed standard list of skills needing to be demonstrated to pass the test in every location.

  F   Introduction of a pass rate of 50% in each centre.

115 G is a large manufacturer of machinery which purchases oil in large quantities to use in its production processes. The oil is stored in two large tankers, referred to as A and B.

G's inventory manager has been instructed not to tie up too much cash in oil since G is currently experiencing some liquidity problems. Consequently he places orders for the minimum required on an ad hoc basis. G has had to postpone two large machinery orders whilst it waited for an oil delivery. The delay in delivering the orders to G's customers will result in cash penalties for G. Oil suppliers are scarce in G's home country.

The directors are concerned that, in trying to improve the liquidity position of G, they have in fact caused the situation to worsen. They have asked the inventory manager to come up with some practical ideas to prevent reoccurrence of the late delivery but also minimise liquidity risk.

Which of the following actions would be suitable suggestions for the inventory manager to make to the board? Select all that apply.

- A   Invest in a third tanker in order to increase stock holding capacity.
- B   Establish a minimum oil inventory level at which an order will be triggered, taking into account current order requirements.
- C   Negotiate shorter lead times with the oil supplier.
- D   Delay payment to suppliers.
- E   Find a new supplier of oil.

116   H manages a block of luxury flats at a popular coastal resort. The flats are owned by individuals who pay H to market them as holiday rentals as well as maintain them and deal with holiday makers staying in them.

H charges a flat fee for this service and also takes 10% of the holiday rental income from each booking. H insists that the owners of the flats make them available for at least 40 weeks of the year.

Any bills which are incurred for maintenance are charged back to the owners with commission of 15% and H provides a cleaning service between rentals which it also charges owners for.

H recently recruited a new office manager who decided to rearrange the filing system in the office. The manager found several invoices for maintenance work carried out by tradesmen which hadn't been recharged to clients because no specific flat address was recorded on the work done section. The office manager also found a file of invoices labelled 'miscellaneous', all paid but without sufficient detail to recharge to any flat. These invoices were mainly for small value items such as toiletries.

H's new office manager wishes to implement a new control system to ensure all costs incurred in maintaining the flats are recharged with commission to owners.

Which of the following controls would reduce the risk of costs not being correctly recharged to flat owners? Select all that apply.

- A   Tradesmen to be paid only on receipt of a completed standardised form showing details of flat number and work done.
- B   Internally generated and sequentially numbered 'goods or service received' notes to be matched to each invoice before payment.
- C   Flat owners to be charged a set amount each year to cover 'miscellaneous' items.
- D   Checks carried out at the end of each month to ensure that all invoices received have been charged to a specific flat.
- E   Any uncharged amounts at the end of each month to be split and recharged equally to all flats.

OBJECTIVE TEST QUESTIONS : SECTION 1

117 Q is a local council department which commissions services from outside contractors to carry out all aspects of the councils work. Q has a list of recommended contractors, many of whom have worked for the council for many years and provide an excellent service at a reasonable price.

Recently, central government announced changes to the health and safety laws in Q's home country. These changes meant that in order to use outside contractors, Q would need to pay for expensive insurance, or insist that contractors apply for a new Health and Safety accreditation certificate. Q does not have a budget to pay for the insurance and to qualify for the certificate contractors must pay for and attend a week long course. As yet, these courses are not available anywhere local to Q.

Central government insists that the new laws will prevent unscrupulous contractors carrying out work without proper safety controls in place. This has been a problem in some areas of the country and led to expensive compensation claims.

Which of the following are risks to Q arising from the changes to health and safety laws? Select all that apply.

A   Q's contractor costs may increase.

B   Q may no longer be able to use recommended contractors.

C   There may be a shortage of contractors for Q to use leading to a backlog of work building up.

D   Q may be unable to obtain the relevant insurance.

E   Incidences of expensive compensation claims may continue to rise.

C2: RISK MANAGEMENT STRATEGIES AND INTERNAL CONTROLS

118 The following are all types of control within an organisation:

(i)   Logical access controls

(ii) Database controls

(iii) Hierarchical passwords

(iv) Range checks

Which of the above controls help to ensure the security of highly confidential information?

A   (i) and (ii) only

B   (i) and (iii) only

C   (i), (ii) and (iii) only

D   All of the above

SUBJECT P3 : RISK MANAGEMENT

119 Foney Ltd has recently experienced a downturn in sales of their own-brand Vodka. The Marketing Director has approached the board of directors with his idea to reinvigorate the sales demand. He has suggested that the company invests in new packaging and re-brand the Vodka to look exactly like a leading well-known brand of vodka, even using their name but selling the product to small off licenses for half the price charged by the market leader.

Which ONE following courses of actions would you suggest to the Board of Foney Ltd?

A   Implement the Marketing Director's idea as it makes strategic sense.

B   Do not proceed as it is too costly.

C   Do not proceed as the situation described by the Marketing Director is counterfeiting.

D   Do not proceed as the situation described by the Marketing Director is embezzlement.

120 Jack, a CIMA member, has recently taken a fantastic position as finance manager for a medium-sized fashion retail company, Acia clothing plc. Jack really enjoys the job and even though the remuneration is not great, the other managers at the company have explained the way they 'get around' that issue. The sales manager explains to Jack that the key is to 'put everything on expenses – private petrol, drinks and even clothing, It's all fine and as long as you have a receipt, no-one in the finance department will question it'. He continues that 'It's fine because the board are aware of it and turn a blind eye'.

Which ONE of the following essential internal control measures is evidently missing from this company?

A   Acia lacks a control environment, Acia are without a board setting an ethical tone at the top

B   Acia lacks an Internal Audit department

C   Acia lacks an experienced finance manager

D   Acia lacks an external auditor

121 Silvermans plc, a large investment bank, has just been involved in a highly publicised fraud investigation concerning the secretary of the Board of Directors.

The investigation found that the secretary had managed to steal £2 million from the directors after they had entrusted her with their chequebooks to settle all personal and professional financial affairs. Within a year the secretary was forging the directors' signatures and transferring monies into her private account

Which ONE of the three prerequisites for fraud had the bosses allowed to flourish within this situation?

A   Rationalisation

B   Motive

C   Greed

D   Opportunity

OBJECTIVE TEST QUESTIONS : **SECTION 1**

122 Fraud risk, such as false accounting or theft of cash or assets, is one component of which type of risk?

   A   Strategic risk

   B   Operational risk

   C   Financial risk

   D   All of above

123 The Finance Director of X plc recently attended a CPD seminar entitled 'Fraud – How to design an anti-fraud strategy'. Her original understanding of her fiduciary duty regarding fraud was that it was her job to detect any wrong doing. However the seminar enabled her to understand there are other aspects to an anti-fraud strategy.

   Which of the following components are key to an effective anti-fraud strategy? Select all that apply.

   A   Prevention

   B   Deterrence

   C   Response

   D   Control

124 Aggrico Bank plc has just employed a new Chief Executive Officer (CEO) after the departing Chief was convicted of a high level fraud. The new CEO has said that she is committed to developing a sound ethical culture to ensure the long-term survival of the bank.

   Which of the following policies would help the new CEO to achieve her aim? Select all that apply.

   A   Establish clear anti-fraud policy statements, with explanations about acceptable behaviour.

   B   A process of reminders to employees regarding fraud policy.

   C   A large redundancy process to removes long-standing employees from the bank.

   D   Establish a route through which suspected fraud can be reported.

125 **The primary responsibility for the prevention and detection of fraud rests with which ONE stakeholder group?**

   A   The Board of Directors

   B   The internal auditors

   C   The external auditors

   D   The Non-Executive Directors

126 Rural Ltd is an independent, small, family-owned construction business that has seen a period of rapid expansion and growth over the last five years. Until now the family have simply relied on informal trust based control systems. However, the finance officer has started to see small inventory discrepancies, the bank reconciliation not quite reconciling and he also suspects internal leaks of client information to a leading competitor.

Which of the following internal control policies would be appropriate for Rural Ltd. to implement? Select all that apply.

- A Fit CCTV cameras in stockrooms
- B Requiring the division of responsibility within the purchasing process – one employee to order goods but another to authorise payment
- C Restricting personal USB drives from being brought into the office environment
- D Calling the National Crime Agency (NCA)

127 X is a hospital. **In the past six months, three of the hospital staff have been attacked when walking home from work late at night. Which of the following controls should reduce the number of attacks?** Select all that apply.

- A Giving all members of staff mobile telephones to report attacks
- B Providing a free bus service for staff finishing work late at night
- C Taking out insurance against attacks on staff
- D Changing the shift pattern, so staff end their shift during daylight
- E Installing floodlighting in the hospital grounds and car parks

128 H has been offering investors in his company a 15% per annum return on their investment. In order to fund this return, H has been using money raised from newer investors to pay the 15% returns demanded by early investors.

What type of fraud is H committing?

- A Manipulation of revenue recognition
- B Advance fee fraud
- C False billing fraud
- D Ponzi scheme

129 BNG Ltd has recently discovered that it has been the victim of a false-billing fraud. Which of the following controls could BNG put in place to prevent this from occurring in the future?

- A Segregation of duties within the accounts department
- B Regular receivables ledger reconciliations
- C Authorisation of payments by management
- D Maintenance of a regular trial balance

130 Fredrickson and Co is a consultancy company that has recently seen the CEO forced to tender her resignation over serious fraud allegations. The rest of the board are looking to regain shareholder confidence.

Identify the THREE main fraud prevention strategies you would recommend to the Board.

- A Create and publish a whistle blowing policy
- B No nothing, as most shareholders will probably be uninterested
- C Create a sound system of internal control
- D Create a culture that is anti-fraud with an anti-fraud 'tone at the top'
- E Announce a special dividend to be paid to all shareholders
- F Dismiss any employee who directly reported to the CEO just in case they might have been involved in any wrong doing

131 S is a multinational oil company which manages hundreds of drilling facilities across the world. S has recently undertaken a risk review of one of its major oil pipelines and as a result is keen to implement some internal control changes in order to reduce costs.

The pipeline in question runs through a remote and inhospitable country which is largely covered in ice. The pipeline is currently checked for corrosion, along its' entire length, once a week. Any signs of corrosion are treated immediately by the maintenance team carrying out the checks. If corrosion were to go untreated, the pipeline may leak resulting in catastrophic damage to the environment.

S's risk assessment suggests that instead of checking the entire pipe for corrosion each week, shorter segments should be checked instead. If the segment checked is clear of corrosion, the chances are the rest of the pipe is also clear. Over the course of a month, the entire pipe would be checked via the segment method.

The directors are very pleased with the cost savings the new internal control system will generate. The chief engineer who manages the maintenance teams is however very concerned at what he perceives to be a dangerous reduction in controls. In his opinion, the risk of corrosion to the pipe is increasing as the pipe gets older and therefore extra checks should be commissioned, rather than checks reduced.

The chief engineer has asked to speak to the board about his concerns.

Which of the following statements are relevant and so should be part of the discussion?
Select all that apply.

- A Potential catastrophic damage to the environment caused by poor controls would increase reputation risk for S.
- B Reduced controls give the impression to maintenance staff that the risks are reduced.
- C Reporting to management on corrosion will no longer be able to take place weekly.
- D Controls should be carried out as cheaply as possible.
- E Corrosion checks should not have been considered as part of a risk assessment.

SUBJECT P3 : RISK MANAGEMENT

132 At a recent board meeting, the directors of R Co were discussing internal controls. The finance director was of the opinion that as long as controls were working over the recording of transactions, there was no need to implement them elsewhere in the business.

The operations director agreed, saying that controls were a financial concern and the factory floor with all of its machinery worked well because of the recruitment of experienced staff who excelled at their jobs rather than the implementation of controls.

It was true that R Co rarely had problems with machine breakdown, however theft of finished goods inventory had been an issue in the past, as had IT security. There had also been three incidences of apparently experienced staff fabricating employment history in order to get a job at R Co. The CEO argued that these problems could be prevented from happening again with the introduction of new controls but the operational director disagreed saying these examples just represented risks of being in business.

Which of the following controls, if implemented, could help prevent one or more of the incidences described from reoccurring? Select all that apply.

- A   Quality and quantity checks on receipt of raw materials before goods receipt notes signed.
- B   Key pad protected access to all inventory storage areas with frequent code changes.
- C   References from two most recent jobs requested and checked for all new recruits.
- D   Individual password protected access to all computer systems with passwords changed frequently.
- E   Quality checks on finished goods before delivery to customers

133 B Company operates car parks across most of the major cities and airports of Country C. At a recent senior management meeting, one of the area managers with responsibility for 20 car parks stated that he had some concerns about revenue collection in the car parks and also security.

He explained that in some of the car parks, the automatic ticket machines which recorded entrance times of vehicles ran out of paper frequently and cars were unable to enter the car park until they were refilled. This often caused traffic jams on entry at busy times.

In addition, the automatic payment machines at the exits always took payment but often ran out of paper to issue receipts to customers when car parks were busy. Although there were signs on the car park entrances stating that cars were left at customers own risk, the occasional vandalism within car parks was occurring and despite the CCTV installed, customers could be put off using them after hours.

Due to recent redundancies and staff sickness, it was difficult to ensure a member of staff was always on site to deal with these issues when they occurred. Often single car park attendants were left with responsibility for the days takings when waiting for the security firm to collect the cash.

Which of the following control weaknesses are likely to lead directly to lost revenue within the car parks? Select all that apply.

- A   Delay in refilling paper in automatic ticket machines.
- B   Delay in refilling paper in automatic payment machines.
- C   Single member of staff responsible for takings until security firm arrives.
- D   Occasional vandalism to cars.
- E   Staff sickness and redundancies.
- F   Lack of attendant on site at all times.

OBJECTIVE TEST QUESTIONS : SECTION 1

C3: INTERNAL AUDIT

134 Many organisations consider outsourcing their Internal Audit function. Which of the following are ADVANTAGES of doing this? Select all that apply.

- A Specialist skills may be more readily available
- B Risk of staff turnover is passed to the outsourcing firm
- C Better understanding of the organisation's objectives and culture
- D May improve independence
- E Decisions relating to Internal Audit can be based solely on cost

135 Many organisations consider outsourcing their Internal Audit function. Which of the following are DISADVANTAGES of doing this? Select all that apply.

- A Flexibility and availability may not be as high as with an in-house function
- B Decisions relating to Internal Audit may be based solely on cost
- C Increased management time
- D Possible conflict of interest if provided by the external auditors
- E Loss of control over standard of service

136 Internal and external audit have similarities, but several features distinguish between them.

Drag and drop the following distinguishing features into the correct category.

	Internal Audit	External Audit
Required by shareholders		
Required by statute		
Reports to Shareholders and Management		
Reports to Audit Committee or Directors		
Reports on financial statements		
Reports on controls		

137 Jan has been invited to run her company's first Internal Audit department. Jan is currently discussing plans for the department with the Finance Director, who is Jan's existing line manager. The Finance Director has made a number of suggestions but Jan is worried they might contravene Internal Audit Attribute Standards.

For each suggestion identify which Internal Audit Attribute Standards are being contravened, if any:

Suggestion	Internal Audit Attribute Standard contravened
It should not be a problem that Jan has no experience of audit and is only part-qualified.	Independence
The first project for the new department should be to audit the Treasury Department, which Jan currently manages.	Objectivity
Jan, as Head of Internal Audit, should report to the Finance Director.	Professional Care
	None contravened

138 Portland plc has a well-established internal audit department consisting of staff that have an average length of service of six years. The scope of the internal auditors work is determined by the Chief Financial Officer (CFO). For some projects the internal audit teams review their own work.

Which of the following statements are correct?

1 The independence of the internal audit department could be enhanced if another member of the finance team was involved in determining the scope of their work.

2 To eliminate any self-review threats Portland plc could increase expenditure on training so that internal auditors are better able to identify errors in their own work.

3 Staff should be rotated on a regular basis to reduce the familiarity threat associated with the long length of service.

A Both 1 and 2

B 2 only

C Both 1 and 3

D 3 only

139 FTS plc is planning to introduce a new benchmarking procedure as part of internal audit to help identify risk areas but is unsure which type of benchmarking would be most appropriate. It is aware that each type of benchmarking has certain drawbacks.

FTS has identified that ____1____ benchmarking is often difficult to undertake as it is difficult to convince the other party to share information about their operations.

____2____ benchmarking is unlikely to suggest any strategic risks for the whole organisation and is typically only useful where the organisation feels that conformity of service is crucial to its operations.

Finally, ____3____ benchmarking often fails to provide data on the benchmarking company's core functions as it requires the organisation to benchmark itself against an organisation in a different industry.

Use the options below to fill in the missing words in gaps 1, 2 and 3.

A Process

B Internal

C Competitive

140 Which of the following is an example of an analytical review procedure?

A Comparing gross profit margin to the prior year figure to identify significant changes

B Enquiries of management regarding the risks of the business

C Observation of internal control procedures

D Recalculation of a balance

141 Moyles Co operate a chain of car dealerships and has a large internal audit department in place. The management of Moyles Co are keen to increase the range of assignments that internal audit undertake.

Which TWO of the following assignments could the internal audit department of Moyles Co be asked to perform by management?

1   Fill a temporary vacancy in the credit control department on a rotational basis.

2   Under the external auditor's supervision, assist the external auditors by evaluating returns from the receivables circularisation.

3   Implement a new inventory control system.

4   Evaluate the inventory count instructions.

A   1 and 2

B   3 and 4

C   2 and 4

D   1 and 3

142 Carson plc is a small family-run company selling fishing tackle and bait from a small chain of shops. The firm has seen rapid sales growth since engaging in e-commerce via a website and selling via large online auction sites.

The newly appointed Finance Director is the only Board member from outside the family and has suggested it would be a good idea for Carson plc to consider establishing an internal audit department as he has already noticed a large inventory discrepancy for fishing clothing.

Which THREE of the following factors are the main reasons for the need for an internal audit at Carson plc?

A   The fact the board has majority family members

B   If a company is listed on the stock exchange it must have an internal audit

C   The growing scale and variety of selling channels suggests there is a higher risk of error

D   Potential internal control issues are starting to arise

E   The introduction of e-commerce

F   The wish of shareholders

143 B Retail has discovered that staff have been excessively discounting stock for sale to friends and family at 2 stores. This is against B retail's staff policies and procedures. They would like their internal audit department to look into this issue at their other 25 stores.

Which of the following types of audit would be applicable? Select all that apply.

A   Compliance audit

B   Management audit

C   Systems audit

D   Risk based audit

E   Environmental audit

SUBJECT P3 : RISK MANAGEMENT

144 Which of the systems below would be audited as a "systems-based audit"?

- A   Sales ledger system
- B   EPOS (Electronic point of sale) system
- C   Non-current asset recording
- D   All of the above

145 Once an audit is completed an audit report is issued. Which of the following are appropriate features of an audit report? Select all that apply.

- A   Recommendations for action
- B   Audit opinion/grading of the area/system reviewed
- C   Results of tests carried out
- D   Objectives of the audit
- E   Summary of the audit process for this audit

146 The directors of BGT have decided to create an internal audit department and in line with company policy, they are keen to promote staff from within BGT to work in the new department.

The finance director has some reservations about this as he believes that a team made up of internal staff will lack independence. The other directors believe that this drawback will be outweighed by the new department's knowledge of BGT which will enable them to become effective much more quickly. There are however some reservations about the availability of internal candidates.

Which of the following factors are arguments the finance director can use to persuade the board that BGT should recruit external candidates into the new internal audit function? Select all that apply.

- A   External recruits will view BGT with a 'fresh pair of eyes' and so be able to more effectively recognise risk.
- B   External recruits will not be at risk of reviewing their own work.
- C   Internal recruits may find it harder to adopt an attitude of professional scepticism towards their colleagues.
- D   External recruits will have a better balance of skills than internal candidates.
- E   Internal promotion will be quicker.

147 X outsources its internal audit work to a local firm of accountants Z. The manager in Z who is responsible for co-ordinating the work done at X has arranged an annual review meeting with the directors of X to discuss the controls work carried out by Z over the last year and any further projects for Z going forward.

At the meeting, the board of directors explained that two instances of fraud had been discovered by their external auditors during the yearend audit. On both occasions the fraud concerned staff ordering computers for their own use through the company's procurement system. It would seem they were able to do this because the system allowed access without a password and could be operated from any computer in the accounts office.

The directors wished to know why Z had not remedied this control weakness during the review of internal controls commissioned last year.

The manager from Z pointed out that a lack of controls over purchasing had been flagged in their report but that as internal auditors they were not responsible for remedying problems.

The directors are questioning whether to dispense with the services of Z on the basis of this statement.

Which of the following actions could Z have carried out over the last year to reduce the risk of fraud occurring? Select all that apply.

- A   Z could have acted as a deterrent to staff perpetrating fraud.
- B   Z could have suggested improvements to the purchasing system.
- C   Z could have implemented controls to prevent access to the purchasing system without a password.
- D   Z could have detected and investigated fraud.
- E   Z could have provided information to be used in the external audit.

148 GAT is a listed company which manufactures complex engineering products. The organisation has been performing very strongly in some new overseas markets over the last year and consequently sales have increased considerably.

A new system for recording sales is currently being installed to cater for the increased number of transactions within the company. Staff training on the new system has yet to be carried out and the Finance Director has some concerns that the changeover from the old system will result in information being lost.

Until a year ago, GAT employed a qualified accountant as an internal auditor however when he left he was not replaced. The Board are now considering a request from the finance director to set up an internal audit department to help with the new systems and ensure controls over sales are adequate. The board are reluctant to authorise the expense of recruiting internal audit staff.

Which of the following factors are arguments the finance director can use to persuade the board that GAT should have an internal audit function? Select all that apply.

- A   Internal audit can manage the sales function and ensure sales are not understated.
- B   Shareholders will be reassured by the presence of internal audit.
- C   Internal audit can help with the systems changeover and work to ensure controls over sales are robust.
- D   Not replacing the internal auditor a year ago contravened listing rules.
- E   GAT has grown in size and become more complex. This suggests it will require more monitoring going forward to reduce risks of fraud and error.

MANAGING RISKS ASSOCIATED WITH CASH FLOWS

D1: EVALUATE FINANCIAL RISKS FACING AN ORGANISATION.

149 For which of the following reasons do exchange rates fluctuate? Select all that apply.

  A Changes in the balance of payments

  B Government policy

  C Developments in Information Technology

  D Speculation

  E Capital movements between economies

150 'There is a risk that the value of our foreign currency-denominated assets and liabilities will change when we prepare our accounts.'

  To which risk does the above statement refer?

  A Translation risk

  B Economic risk

  C Transaction risk

  D Interest rate risk

151 Eady plc is a UK company that imports furniture from a Canadian supplier and sells it throughout Europe. Eady plc has just received a shipment of furniture, invoiced in Canadian dollars, for which payment is to be made in two months' time. Neither Eady plc nor the Canadian supplier use hedging techniques to cover their exchange risk.

  If the pound sterling were to weaken substantially against the Canadian dollar, what would be the foreign exchange gain or loss effects upon Eady plc and the Canadian supplier?

	Eady plc	*Canadian supplier*
A	Gain	No effect
B	No effect	Gain
C	Loss	No effect
D	Loss	Gain

152 In periods of rising inflation, commodities can act as a hedge to a portfolio of shares and bonds because the:

  A Commodities will not be affected by a rise in inflation.

  B Commodities will typically appreciate in price when prices of stocks and bonds decline.

  C Commodities can provide current income to offset any price decreases in shares and bonds.

  D Decreases in price of commodities.

OBJECTIVE TEST QUESTIONS : SECTION 1

153 The interest rate risk of a bond is the:

A   risk related to the possibility of bankruptcy of the bond's issuer.

B   unsystematic risk caused by factors unique in the bond.

C   risk related to the possibility of bankruptcy of the bond's issuer, which arises from the uncertainty of the bond's return caused by the change in interest rates.

D   risk that arises from the uncertainty about the bond's return caused by changes in interest rates over time.

154 Political risk analysis is conducted by a company considering international operations and normally focuses on the:

A   world economy generally

B   relations between the USA, Japan and Europe

C   political and cultural differences between the home and target country

D   industrialisation of the target country

155 When using the expected value criterion, it is assumed that the individual wants to

A   maximise return for a given level of risk

B   maximise return irrespective of the level of risk

C   minimise risk for a given level of return

D   minimise risk irrespective of the level of return

156 A company has constructed a model for predicting profits. Net profit or loss depends on two variables: gross profit and overheads. The following are independent probability distributions of the two variables.

Gross profit	Probability	Overheads	Probability
12,000	0.1	6,000	0.3
6,000	0.4	4,000	0.3
4,000	0.4	3,000	0.3
3,000	0.1	2,000	0.1

What is the probability that the company will make a positive net profit?

A   0.27

B   0.55

C   0.73

D   0.82

SUBJECT P3 : RISK MANAGEMENT

157 Joe is supervisor of the Receivables Team at X Ltd. He has been told that he is responsible for managing 'credit risk'.

Identify which THREE of the following directly determine the level of credit risk to which X is exposed.

A The total volume of sales

B The total volume of credit sales

C The time allowed to customers to pay

D Debt collection procedures

E Joe's management style

158 **Company P has decided to finance its foreign investment through local finance. Which of the following statements is correct?** Select all that apply.

A Local financing can minimise translation risk

B Local financing can minimise transaction risk

C Local financing can minimise interest rate risk

D Local financing is dependent on the state of the banking and capital markets of the country concerned

E Local financing reduces the risk of P's assets being confiscated

D2: EVALUATE ALTERNATIVE RISK MANAGEMENT TOOLS.

EXCHANGE RATE THEORY AND VALUE AT RISK

159 Inflation in the UK is 5%p.a. and in the US is 6%p.a. Given that the spot rate is currently GBP 1 = USD 1.5000.

What will a UK company have to pay in Sterling, in 12 months, to buy a commodity costing $10,000 (assuming Purchasing Power Parity)? (Answer to the nearest GBP).

£_____

160 Interest rates in the UK are forecast to be 2% over the next year and 3% in the Eurozone. The current spot rate is GBP 1 = EUR 1.25.

Determine the exchange rate in one year (assuming Interest Rate Parity). (Give your answer in the form GBP 1 = EUR... working to 4 dp).

_____

161 Interest Rate Parity Theory generally holds true in practice. However it suffers from several limitations.

Which of the following is not a limitation of Interest Rate Parity Theory?

A Government controls on capital markets

B Controls on currency trading

C Intervention in foreign exchange markets

D Future inflation rates are only estimates

162 In Country A inflation is predicted to be 5% and (nominal) interest rates are 11.3%. In Country B interest rates are 13.42%.

Assuming the International Fischer effect holds, determine the expected inflation rate in Country B. (Give your answer as a percentage to 1 decimal place)

_____

163 The current spot exchange rate between sterling and the Euro is EUR 1.4415/GBP. The sterling three month interest rate is 5.75% pa and the Euro three month interest rate is 4.75% pa.

What should the three month EUR/GBP forward rate be?

A 1.4553

B 1.4379

C 1.4279

D 1.4451

164 X is a bank. The management accountant of X has estimated that the value of its asset portfolio at year end will be $1,200 million, with a standard deviation of $430 million.

Calculate the value at risk of the portfolio, at a 95% confidence level. (Express your answer in $, rounded to the nearest million.)

$_____

165 The current spot exchange rate between sterling and the dollar is USD 1.3127/GBP. The sterling nine month interest rate is 1.75% pa and the dollar nine month interest rate is 1.40% pa.

What should the nine month USD/GBP forward rate be?

A 1.3093

B 1.3172

C 1.3082

D 1.3161

166 Biskit Co, a UK based company, has sold goods on credit to an American customer. They have invoiced in dollars for 10 million.

The exchange rate is currently 1.2785 USD to the £.

The daily volatility of the pound/dollar exchange rate is 0.75%.

Calculate to the nearest £1,000, the 1-day 97.5% VAR.

£ _____

FOREIGN EXCHANGE RATE RISK MANAGEMENT

167 Edted plc has to pay a Spanish supplier EUR 100,000 in three months' time. The company's Finance Director wishes to avoid exchange rate exposure, and is looking at four options.

(1) Do nothing for three months and then buy Euros at the spot rate.

(2) Pay in full now, buying Euros at today's spot rate.

(3) Buy Euros now, put them on deposit for three months, and pay the debt with these Euros plus accumulated interest.

(4) Arrange a forward exchange contract to buy the euros in three months' time.

Which of these options would provide cover against the exchange rate exposure that Edted would otherwise suffer?

A   Option (4) only

B   Options (3) and (4) only

C   Options (2), (3) and (4) only

D   Options (1), (2), (3) and (4)

168 Which of the following measures will allow a UK company to enjoy the benefits of a favourable change in exchange rates for their Euro receivables contracts while protecting them from unfavourable exchange rate movements? Select all that apply.

A   A forward exchange contract

B   A put option for Euros

C   A call option for Euros

D   A money market hedge

169 Methods for hedging foreign currency risk can be classified as either 'internal' or 'external'. Drag and drop the following hedging methods into the correct category.

	Internal	External
Forward contracts		
Futures		
Leading and lagging		
Matching and netting		
Options		
Countertrade		

170 There are different methods that can be used to internally hedge foreign exchange risk. Match the examples below to the appropriate method.

Method	Example
Matching	Transferring all bank account balances in one currency into a single account
Netting	Exchanging goods or services of similar value
Pooling	Financing a foreign investment with a foreign currency loan
Countertrade	Using a foreign currency receipt to offset a foreign currency payment

171 The following options are held by Frances plc at their expiry date:

(1) A call option on GBP 500,000 in exchange for USD at an exercise price of GBP 1 = USD 1.90. The exchange rate at the expiry date is GBP 1 = USD 1.95.

(2) A put option on GBP 400,000 in exchange for Singapore Dollars at an exercise price of GBP 1 = SGD 2.90. The exchange rate at the expiry date is GBP 1 = SGD 2.95.

Which one of the following combinations (exercise/lapse) should be undertaken by the company?

	Call	Put
A	Exercise	Lapse
B	Exercise	Exercise
C	Lapse	Exercise
D	Lapse	Lapse

172 SGB Ltd in the UK have sold USD 5m worth of goods to AW Inc. in the US, they are considering hedging the contract using options.

The current spot is £/$1.5500 and the option strike price is GBP 1 = USD 1.6000 the contract size is GBP 25,000 per contract and the premium is USD 1,000 per contract.

What is the GBP value of the premium that SGB must pay?

A   80,645

B   83,226

C   125,000

D   129,000

173 X (a UK company) has purchased goods for USD 50,000 and payment is due in 30 days. The current spot rate for USD is GBP1/USD 1.5500 – 1.5400 and the one month forward contract is priced at 0.50-0.30 cpm.

Calculate the amount of GBP that X will pay under the forward contract (to the nearest GBP).

£_____

SUBJECT P3 : RISK MANAGEMENT

174 X (a UK company) must pay EUR 1 million to a Spanish supplier in six months' time. The treasurer of X has obtained the following information:

- Spot rate GBP 1/EUR 1.2000 – 1.1950
- EUR borrowing can be obtained at 4.0%p.a. and deposits pay 2.0%p.a.
- GBP borrowing can be obtained at 5.0%p.a. and deposits pay 3.0%p.a.

Calculate the cost to X in GBP of a money market hedge, to the nearest GBP. (Round calculations to the nearest GBP or EUR, at each stage of the calculation).

£_____

175 DWTV Inc. a US company has purchased goods from T2 in the UK at a cost of GBP 25 Million. They have taken out an option at a strike price of GBP 1 = 1.6700 USD with a premium of USD 85,000. When the contract is closed out the spot rate is 1.6850.

What is the USD cost of the purchase to DWTV Inc?

$_____

176 Pogs has a long position (that is, it has bought) 2,000 December long gilt contracts. Each contract is for £500 and the tick size is 1/16.

The contract position fell from 119 8/16 to 118 15/16.

What is the profit or loss on the futures contract?

£_____

177 SOMH Ltd, a company based in the United States, is to receive EUR 700,000 from Pops Plc who are based in Germany in 6 months' time. The treasurer of SOMH intends to use the forward market to hedge the risk exposure on the transaction.

The spot rate is USD1: EUR 1.7027 – 1.6231

The 6 months forward rate is priced at 2.50 – 1.50 cdis

How much will SOMH receive in USD, using a forward contract?

A   435,296.31

B   427,324.34

C   417,237.89

D   405,162.93

178 APS Plc is based in the UK, they have recently sold a significant amount of goods to RJS in France. APS have agreed to invoice in EUR and the total invoice amount is EUR 1,200,000. APS are concerned that the value of sterling will rise so they have taken out an option at a strike price of GBP1= EUR 1.4405 and a premium of GBP 35,000.

When the transaction is closed, the spot rate is GBP1 = 1.4640.

What is the net sterling value in GBP of the contract to APS Plc?

£_____

179

Money market hedge for ZZB (US company paying GBP):
- Deposit GBP now: £6,000,000 / 1.025 = £5,853,658.54
- Buy GBP with USD at spot 0.9610: $5,853,658.54 / 0.9610 = $6,091,216
- Borrow USD at 11% p.a. (5.5% for 6 months): $6,091,216 × 1.055 = $6,426,233

$6,426,000

180 D £217,647

Contracts needed = $4,000,000 / ($1.45 × £25,000) = 110.34 → 111 contracts
Premium = 111 × $2,500 = $277,500
In GBP = $277,500 / $1.2750 = £217,647

181 A and D

- Short position, price fell → **profit** (A correct)
- Price movement: 124 53/64 − 121 8/64 = 3 45/64 = 237/64
- Profit per contract = 237 × £500 × (1/64) = £1,851.5625
- Total profit = 1,000 × £1,851.5625 = **£1,851,563** (D correct)

182 The following options are held by Xavier plc at their expiry date:

(1) A call option on GBP 800,000 in exchange for EUR at an exercise price of GBP 1 = EUR 1.2000. The exchange rate at the expiry date is GBP 1 = EUR 1.1500.

(2) A put option on GBP 1,000,000 in exchange for dollars at an exercise price of GBP 1 = USD 1.3000. The exchange rate at the expiry date is GBP 1 = USD 1.2500.

Which one of the following combinations (exercise/lapse) should be undertaken by the company?

	Call	Put
A	Exercise	Lapse
B	Exercise	Exercise
C	Lapse	Exercise
D	Lapse	Lapse

INTEREST RATE RISK MANAGEMENT

183 When hedging interest rate risk, a variety of instruments are available. Match the instruments below with the relevant descriptions.

Instrument		Description	
A	Forward Rate Agreement (FRA)	1	A traded instrument, hedging only downside risk
B	Interest Rate Guarantee (IRG)	2	A traded instrument, with a fixed rate
C	Future	3	An over the counter instrument, with a fixed rate
D	Option	4	An over the counter instrument, hedging only downside risk

184 X (a company) wishes to borrow $1 million in three months, for a period of six months. A bank has quoted the following (Forward Rate Agreement) FRA rates:

3 v 9   5.55 – 5.70

X can borrow at 0.50% above base rate, and the base rate is currently 4.50%. Concerned that base rates may rise, X decides to take the FRA offered by the bank.

At the settlement date for the FRA, base rate has risen to 6.00%. What is the effective interest rate paid by X, for its borrowing? (Answer in %, to 2 decimal places).

%

185 The owner of an interest-rate cap will

A receive a payment if the market rate exceeds the cap rate

B receive a payment if the market rate is less than the cap rate

C be required to make a payment if the market rate exceeds the cap rate

D be required to make a payment if the market rate is less than the cap rate

OBJECTIVE TEST QUESTIONS : SECTION 1

186 DD Co has a floating rate borrowing with an interest rate of LIBOR + 1.5%.

The directors are concerned that interest rates are forecast to rise, so they have approached their bank to discuss the possibility of entering an interest rate swap.

The bank has quoted swap rates of 4.9% – 5% against LIBOR.

If DD Co enters the swap arrangement, what net interest rate will it pay?

- A   LIBOR + 5%
- B   5%
- C   6.4%
- D   6.5%

187 Company A would like to take out a variable rate loan for a new project. Company B also has a new project but would like to take out a fixed rate loan in order to have certainty over interest payments.

Company A has been quoted a fixed rate of 7% and a variable rate of LIBOR + 4%. Company B has been quoted a fixed rate of 6% and a variable rate of LIBOR + 2% as it has a higher credit rating than A.

If they enter into a swap arrangement, agreeing to split gains equally, what effective rate will each end up paying?

- A   Co A   7%   Co B   LIBOR + 2%
- B   Co A   LIBOR + 4%   Co B   6%
- C   Co A   LIBOR + 2%   Co B   7%
- D   Co A   LIBOR + 3.5% Co B   5.5%

188 Grudem plc needs to borrow USD 12 million in 6 months' time as is concerned about interest rate risk exposure.

Which of the following strategies would help Grudem manage this risk? Select all that apply.

- A   Sell FRAs
- B   Buy put options on short term interest rate futures
- C   Buy an interest rate cap
- D   Buy bond futures

189 Match how you would calculate the value of the net payment or receipt of interest in each of the following situations:

Situation
Company has a loan and a cap where the strike rate is higher than the market rate
Company has a deposit and a floor where the strike rate is higher than the market rate
Company has a loan and a cap where the strike rate is less than the market rate
Company has a deposit and a floor where the strike rate is less than the market rate

Calculations
Strike rate + premium costs
Market rate + premium costs
Strike rate – premium costs
Market rate – premium costs

190 Match which option or combination of options would be needed to achieve the following required risk positions:

Required position	Combination of options
A 'cap' on the interest rate on a loan	Buy a Put on a FRA and sell a call on a FRA
A 'floor' on the interest rate on a deposit	Buy a Call on a FRA
A 'collar' to protect the interest cost of a loan	Buy a Call on a FRA and sell a put on a FRA
A 'collar' to protect the interest on a deposit	Buy a Put on a FRA

191 An interest rate option is:

   A   A right but not an obligation to buy or sell interest rate futures

   B   An obligation to obtain a loan at an agreed interest rate at a future date

   C   A right but not an obligation to obtain a loan at a future date

   D   A right but not an obligation to an agreed interest rate on a notional loan

192 Which of the following statements are true for an interest rate floor? Select all that apply.

   A   Can be achieved by buying a call on a FRA

   B   Is useful where a company is concerned about the cost of a loan

   C   Is useful when interest rates are thought likely to fall

   D   Will effectively reduce the interest rate on a deposit because of the premium costs

   E   Guarantees the minimum value of a loan

193 According to the Black-Scholes model, five variables affect the price of a call option.

   Which of the following are components of the Black-Scholes model? Select all that apply.

   A   The spot price of the underlying asset

   B   The tax rate

   C   The variability of the price of the underlying asset

   D   The time to maturity

   E   The risk free interest rate

194 Most futures contracts are closed through which ONE of the following:

   A   delivery

   B   arbitrage

   C   a reversing trade

   D   an exchange-for-physicals

195 Which one of the following statements regarding Over-the-Counter derivatives is true?

    A   They carry no default risk

    B   They are customized contracts

    C   They are backed by the OTC Clearinghouse

    D   They have good liquidity in the over-the-counter (OTC) market

196 Which of the following is least likely to be described as a benefit of derivatives markets?

    A   Derivatives markets help keep interest rates down

    B   Derivatives markets supply valuable price information

    C   Derivatives allow the shifting of risk to those who can most efficiently bear it

    D   Transactions costs are usually smaller in derivatives markets than for similar trades in the underlying asset

197 Pick three advantages of options from the list of properties below:

    A   Provide complete certainty as to the amount to be paid or received

    B   Simple to understand and cheap to operate

    C   Provide a means of hedging uncertain transactions

    D   Guaranteed conformance to hedge accounting requirements

    E   Provide a guaranteed minimum sum received or maximum sum paid

    F   Ensure that the cash flows associated with financing the transaction are known in advance

198 A company are looking to take out a loan in 6 months' time for a period of 9 months. LIBOR is currently 3% and the bank has quoted them L + 0.55 on the following forward rates for LIBOR:

7 V 16   3.5 – 3.75

6 V 15   3.45 – 3.7

What is the effective rate that the company will pay?

    A   4.30%

    B   4.25%

    C   4.05%

    D   4.00%

SUBJECT P3: RISK MANAGEMENT

199 M Plc and D plc would like to borrow the same amount of money. M plc has been in existence for a long time, while D has only recently set up. They have agreed to enter into a swap for mutual benefit. Any benefits will be split in the ratio 60:40 in M's favour.

M plc can borrow at 7% fixed and variable at LIBOR +2%.

D plc can borrow at 8% fixed and variable at LIBOR +3.3%.

M would like to end up with a fixed rate exposure, while D would like a variable rate exposure.

If M and D enter into a swap, which TWO are the correct effective loan rates?

- A M will pay a fixed rate of 7.82%
- B M will pay a fixed rate of 6.82%
- C M will pay a variable rate of LIBOR + 3.18%
- D M will pay a variable rate of LIBOR + 1.82%
- E D will pay a fixed rate of 7.82%
- F D will pay a variable rate of LIBOR + 3.18%
- G D will not want to enter into a swap.

200 Company C is looking to borrow money at the moment, they are considering interest options. The current rate is 5.25%, but forecasts suggest it will rise. They can get an option at 5.5%, the option has a premium of 0.85% and a price of 94.5 (100 – 5.5).

The premium is higher than C would like to pay and have been reviewing how they could reduce the premium. They are considering an option that the bank has priced at 95.05 with a premium of 0.34%.

If Company C were to set up a collar arrangement, which of the following would be true?
Select all that apply.

- A The premium would be 1.19%
- B The ceiling would be 5.50%
- C The ceiling would be 5.05%
- D The floor would be 5.05%
- E The floor would be 4.95%
- F The premium would be 0.51%

201 UB50 have a variable rate loan at L + 4.5%

They are concerned that rates may rise and are investigating the possibility of a swap.

The bank has quoted 7.4 – 7.5% against LIBOR.

Which if the following are correct? Select all that apply.

- A The bid rate is 7.4%
- B The bid rate is 7.5%
- C The ask rate is 7.4%
- D The ask rate is 7.5%
- E The effective rate the UB50 will pay is 11.9%
- F The effective rate the UB50 will pay is 12%

OBJECTIVE TEST QUESTIONS : SECTION 1

202 The owner of an interest-rate floor will

- A receive the lowest possible rate of interest on a loan
- B receive a payment if the market rate is less than the floor rate
- C reduce the premium paid on an interest cap on a deposit.
- D be required to make a payment if the market rate is less than the floor rate

203 Tither plc needs to deposit GBP 6 million in 12 months' time and is concerned about interest rate risk exposure.

Which of the following strategies would help Tither manage this risk? Select all that apply.

- A Sell FRAs
- B Matching
- C Buy put options on short term interest rate futures
- D Buy an interest rate cap
- E Buy bond futures
- F Smoothing

MANAGING RISKS ASSOCIATED WITH CAPITAL INVESTMENT DECISIONS

E1: INVESTMENT APPRAISAL

204 The Adjusted Present Value (APV) method of project appraisal should be used when capital structure is expected <DROP DOWN BOX> as a result of the project.

- A not to change
- B to change a little
- C to change significantly

205 Which of the following conditions are necessary for a company to use the pre-project company weighted average cost of capital (WACC) as a discount rate for project appraisal? Select all that apply.

- A The capital structure will change, as a result of the project
- B The project carries a different level of business risk from the company's existing operations
- C The new investment is large, in comparison to the capital of the company
- D The company will raise additional finance to maintain its current gearing ratio
- E The WACC is above bank base rate

SUBJECT P3 : RISK MANAGEMENT

206 A decision-maker wishes to use certainty equivalents as part of a net present value (NPV) calculation. What is the appropriate discount rate to use in such an approach?

    A   the company's cost of debt

    B   the company's cost of equity

    C   the company's WACC

    D   the risk free rate

    E   the bank base rate

207 SCW plc makes equipment for a range of countryside activities, including camping, hunting, shooting and fishing. It is currently financed purely by equity. The FD is currently assessing four new investment opportunities.

Select the best investment appraisal technique for each of the investment scenarios given (Note: you can choose the same technique more than once if you wish)

Projects
A – Develop a new range of light weight crossbows. Finance by cutting the forthcoming dividend.
B – Diversify into making luxury yachts. Finance to be raised to maintain the current gearing ratio.
C – Develop a new range of weapons for the police force of Country P. SCW can access a subsidized loan as part of the proposal.
D – Building a new range of fly fishing reels. Finance to be raised via a rights issue.

Techniques
Adjusted Present Value
Calculate a NPV using a risk-adjusted WACC
Calculate a NPV using the existing company WACC as a discount rate

208 The higher risk of a project can be incorporated into investment appraisal by decreasing

    A   The cost of the initial investment of the project

    B   The estimates of future cash inflows from the project

    C   The internal rate of return of the project

    D   The required rate of return of the project

209 Zodhiates plc is looking at different alternatives for building its new factory and has decided to design it around modules with general purpose plant and machinery rather than a more traditional specialised production line.

Which ONE of the following real options is included within the factory decision?

    A   Option to abandon

    B   Option to delay

    C   Option to follow on

    D   Option to return

OBJECTIVE TEST QUESTIONS : SECTION 1

210 X (a company) is considering an investment project that requires a $3 million investment. The risk free rate is 8%, and the directors are 95% certain that cash savings will be made in perpetuity.

Calculate the annual cash saving required for the project to break even. (Answer in $, rounded to the nearest $)

$_____

211 Which of the following parties is least likely to benefit from capital investment decisions that increase risk and expected return for a company?

- A Creditors
- B Chief executive officers
- C Chief financial officers
- D Shareholders

212 Y Ltd is a small, family-owned car sales company, currently financed by a mixture of debt and equity. The shareholders do not have any other investments. The company is looking into investing in a new, bigger car showroom. The financing for the investment will be from internally generated funds.

Which ONE of the following investment appraisal calculations would be appropriate for Y Ltd to use to assist with the decision-making process?

- A The company's existing Weighted Average Cost of Capital
- B The company's existing Cost of Equity
- C Adjusted Present Value appraisal
- D Capital Asset Pricing Model

213 Sonil, is a management accountant for a Z plc a listed international car sales company. It is looking into investing in a new innovative hybrid car. The financing for the investment will be from the issue of a large redeemable debenture which will double the gearing of the company.

Which ONE of the following investment appraisal calculations would be appropriate for Sonil to use as a basis for decision-making?

- A The company's existing Weighted Average Cost of Capital
- B The company's existing Cost of Equity
- C A risk-adjusted Weighted Average Cost of Capital
- D Capital Asset Pricing Model

SUBJECT P3 : RISK MANAGEMENT

214 Manisha, is a management accountant for a K plc a large manufacturing company. She is undertaking an exercise to calculate the Weighted Average Cost of Capital for the company.

Which of the following balances should Manisha include in the 'Debt' balance, when calculating WACC? Select all that apply.

- A   Trade payables
- B   Bank loan
- C   A rarely used bank overdraft
- D   Debenture

215 M plc is a large listed manufacturing company based in the UK and most of its shareholders are investment funds. The production director is considering the proposal of expanding the company's operations into Asia. The finance director has commented that they will need to reassess the company's required return as their existing calculation is based on the capital asset pricing model (CAPM).

Which ONE of the following is most likely to be true about the required return?

- A   The required return will decrease because of a reduction in unsystematic risk due to diversification.
- B   The required return will increase because of a rise in unsystematic risk due to extra risks of the foreign market.
- C   The required return will remain unchanged as the level of systematic risk will not change.
- D   It is impossible to estimate the impact on the required return without further information regarding the relative betas of the different activities.

216 Diversification of unsystematic risk within a portfolio of assets held by the company, is ultimately the responsibility of which stakeholder?

- A   The Finance Director
- B   The Board of directors
- C   A rational investor
- D   The Audit committee

217 The Capital Asset Pricing Model calculates the required rate of return for an individual security.

Which of the following are variables within the CAPM equation? Select all that apply.

- A   The risk free rate of investment
- B   The share price
- C   The average return on the market
- D. The beta factor

OBJECTIVE TEST QUESTIONS : SECTION 1

218 Match the beta value to the relevant required rate of return

Beta Value	Required rate of return
A – Beta value less than one	(i) The shares have more systematic risk than the market average, therefore the investor will require a higher than average return
B – Beta value greater than one	(ii) The shares have the same systematic risk as the market average, therefore the investor will require an average return
C – Beta value equal to zero	(iii) The shares have less systematic risk than the market average, therefore the investor will require a lower than average return
D – Beta value equal to one	(iv) The shares have no systematic risk, therefore the investor will require a risk free rate of return

219

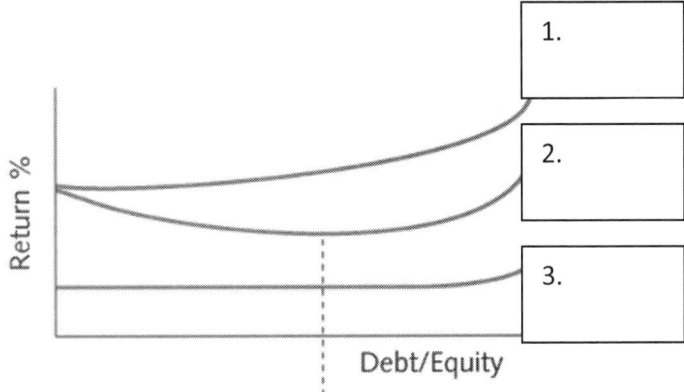

Which ONE of the following CORRECTLY labels the lines on the above graph?

A   1 = Ke, 2 = WACC, 3 = Kd

B   1 = WACC, 2 = Ke, 3 = Kd

C   1 = WACC, 2 = Kd, 3 = Ke

D   1 = Ke, 2 = Kd, 3 = WACC

220 A company has been trading for 10 months and achieved the following monthly profits:

(£5,000)   twice

£1,000   three times

£7,000   four times

£12,000   once

Using an Expected Value calculation, which ONE of the following is the average monthly profit?

    A   £12,000

    B   £7,000

    C   £1,000

    D.   £3,300

221 Which ONE of the following CORRECTLY labels the lines on the following graph?

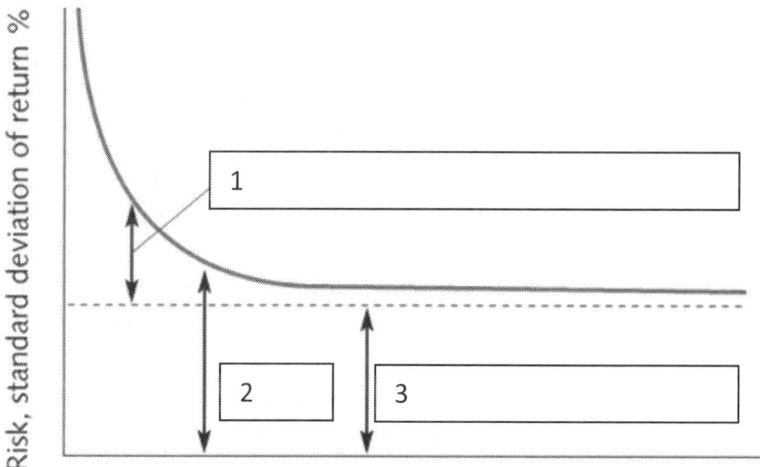

A   1 = Total risk, 2 = Unsystematic risk, 3 = Systematic risk

B   1 = Unsystematic risk, 2 = Systematic risk, 3 = Total risk

C   1 = Unsystematic risk, 2 = Total risk, 3 = Systematic risk

D   1 = Total risk, 2 = Systematic risk, 3 = Unsystematic risk

222 Using your knowledge of the Securities Market Line (SML), recommend which ONE investment would be most suitable for a risk-averse investor who requires an investment only half as risky as the market average?

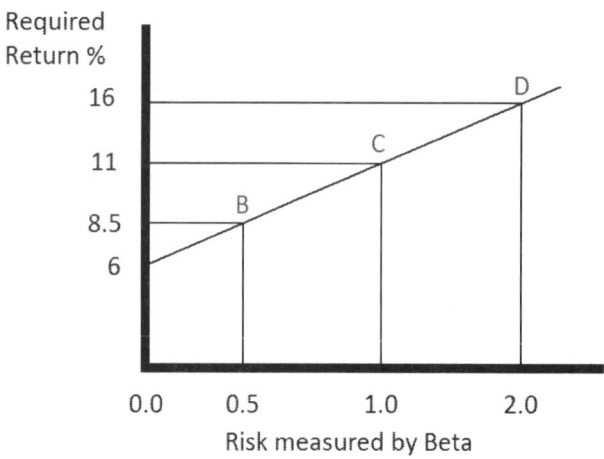

A   Impossible to tell from the information available

B   B

C   C

D   D

OBJECTIVE TEST QUESTIONS : SECTION 1

223 Using the beta values in the table below, which ONE industry would a risk seeking investor be most interested in investing in?

Industry	Beta Value
Water utility	0.33
Tobacco	0.76
Funeral services	0.83
Advertising	1.25

A Water

B Tobacco

C Funeral services

D Advertising

224 Winestones, a national bookselling company, is looking at three different potential scenarios for a project under consideration. The project will require an investment of £100,000, will produce net inflows of £55,000 in year 1 and £70,000 in year 2.

The finance manager has produced the following information:

Scenario	Level of risk	Risk-free rate (%)	Risk premium (%)	Risk-adjusted rate (%)
I	Low	9	+3	12
II	Medium	9	+6	15
III	High	9	+10	19

Using the risk-adjusted rate, which of the scenarios would result in the project being accepted? Select all that apply.

A Scenario I

B Scenario II

C Scenario III

D Impossible to calculate

225 G plc is considering launching a new product. It will launch the new product if the expected value of the total revenue is in excess of $1,000. It was decided to set the selling price at $10 per unit.

After some investigation, a range of probabilities for different levels of sales revenue has been predicted as summarised in the following table:

Units sold	Revenue	Probability
80	$800	0.15
100	$1,000	0.50
120	$1,200	0.35

Using an expected value calculation, which ONE of the following is the expected revenue for G plc?

A $1,000

B $1,200

C $1,040

D $800

69

SUBJECT P3 : RISK MANAGEMENT

226 D plc is considering whether to make product X or product Y but cannot make both products. The estimated sales demand for each product is uncertain and the following probability distribution of the Net Present Values for each product has been identified.

Product X NPV £	Probability (%)
3,000	10
3,500	20
4,000	40
4,500	20
5,000	10

Product Y NPV £	Probability (%)
2,000	5
3,000	10
4,000	40
5,000	25
6,000	20

Using expected values, which ONE of the following would you recommend for D plc?

A   Accept Product X

B   Accept Product Y

C   Accept both Product X and Y

D   Accept neither product X nor Y

227 Jamie Jones runs a busy canteen. Based upon previous demand it is expected that, during the 250-day working year, the canteen will require the following daily quantities:

On 25 days of the year   40 salads

On 50 days of the year   50 salads

On 100 days of the year   60 salads

On 75 days on the days   70 salads

Using the data above, which ONE of the following percentages represents the probability of 70 salads being required?

A   10%

B   20%

C   30%

D   40%

228 Claire, a management accountant at A plc is investigating the company's weighted average cost of capital. She has discovered the capital structure is as follows:

	Cost of Capital %	Book value £m	Market value £m
Bank loans	6	5	5
Debenture loans	10	8	5
Ordinary shares	15	18	30

Using the data above, Which ONE of the following is A plc's weighted average cost of capital?

A 6%

B 10%

C 15%

D 13.25%

229 J plc is a company involved in housing construction. The planning officer has just been informed of a prime piece of real estate soon to become available. After discussion, the Board of J plc has decided to buy the land for £1 million, as the Finance Director is confident that, even if planning permission is not awarded, the future price of the land will only increase and if the company wishes to sell the land in the future it will be able to make a profit.

Which ONE of the following option types would best describe the Finance Director's argument?

A An abandonment real option

B A follow-on real option

C A timing real option

D A financial option

230 Cheetah plc is a UK car sales company. The Sales Director is interested in expanding operation into country X. X is a country with a 20% growth rate in GDP and an emerging consumer economy. The Sales Director wishes to enter country X now. However the Managing Director thinks the better choice would to be to delay entry until country X has had a longer period of political stability and the current extensive road building project is completed.

Which ONE of the following would best describe the managing director's thoughts?

A An abandonment option

B A follow-on option

C A 'wait-and-see' option (timing option)

D A financial option

231 Cleanaway plc, a UK company, manufactures and retails cleaning products. The Marketing Director wishes to sell a new-to-market, innovative mop, which costs £5 to manufacture, for a recommended introductory retail price of £3.99. Her rationale for the loss-leading pricing strategy is that the mop-heads, which need replacing on a regular basis, will be sold for £3, and they cost only 50p to manufacture.

Which ONE of the following would best describes the Marketing Director's thoughts?

   A   An abandonment option

   B   A follow-on option

   C   A 'wait-and-see' option (timing option)

   D   A financial option

232 James, a newly-qualified CIMA accountant, is a new member of staff in the finance team at R plc working in the investment project appraisal team. The current investment appraisal technique is familiar to James, as it is fundamentally modelled on a net present value technique. However, the team has just been asked to evaluate the proposal of a significant relocation of the call centre services from the UK to India. The move will be largely finance by a subsidised loan from the Indian government. James has heard his manager say that a NPV calculation will be used as step one to calculate the base case NPV. However, for this appraisal an adjusted present value technique (APV) is more appropriate which also requires a second step as part of the calculation process.

Which ONE of the following best describes the second step of an APV calculation?

   A   To calculate a new share price for R plc

   B   To calculate the present value of the costs and benefits associated with the finance package

   C   To calculate the sunk costs of the relocation

   D   To calculate the redundancy cost of the relocation

233 When performing an adjusted present value appraisal, it is necessary to consider separately the financing costs and benefits associated with a new project.

Which of the following costs and benefits would be considered relevant? Select all that apply.

   A   The present value of costs to issue the new financing

   B   The present value of new total interest payments to be incurred

   C   The present value of the tax shield gained on interest payment

   D   The present value of dividends

234 Which of the ONE of the following is the generally accepted primary strategic objective of a commercial company?

   A   The maximisation of a company's profit

   B   The maximisation of shareholders wealth

   C   The pursuit of new opportunities

   D   The sustained employment of the work force

OBJECTIVE TEST QUESTIONS : SECTION 1

235 X plc is a well-known clothing brand which has always sourced its clothes from the UK. However it is now considering importing its merchandise from abroad, where the clothing lines can be made at a much lower cost. X plc is also thinking of acquiring a manufacturing subsidiary based in an emerging market.

Based upon the available information, match the stakeholders of X plc with their potentially conflicting goals:

Stakeholder		Goals	
A	Equity investors	(i)	The value for money of products must at least remain, if not improve
B	Customers	(ii)	The strategy will need to result in a higher return
C	Employees	(iii)	The partnership will end
D	UK suppliers	(iv)	Long term security of X plc

236 Z plc is an electrical appliances manufacturer. The production director has managed to source a key electrical component for half the price Z plc is currently paying. However, the component, once included in the appliance, will only last half of the time of the current component before it needs to be replaced.

Which of the following conflicts between stakeholder objectives may occur? Select all that apply.

- A Long-term customer satisfaction conflicting with a short-term increase in profit
- B Long term shareholder wealth conflicting with a short-term increase in profit
- C Long term reduction in market share conflicting with a short-term increase in profit
- D Long term brand reputation damage conflicting with a short-term increase in profit

237 Mr Big, the chief executive officer of K plc has just left a meeting with the board of G plc, a market leader in the same industry. The board of G plc have just made an informal bid for K plc offering a premium of 30% above current market value for K's shares. This is a fantastic opportunity for K's shareholders to increase their wealth. However the deal will only apply if Mr Big relinquishes his office. Mr Big has decided to try to dissuade the shareholders of K from accepting the offer.

Which of the following courses of action are appropriate for Mr Big to follow? Select all that apply.

- A Mr Big could start a publicity campaign against G plc to try to stop the shareholders of K plc selling their holdings
- B Mr Big could call an extraordinary general meeting to explain the offer
- C Mr Big could start buying up shares in K plc
- D Mr Big could discuss the offer with the non-executive directors of K plc

SUBJECT P3 : RISK MANAGEMENT

238 A definition of goal congruence within a control system is 'the state which leads individuals or groups to take actions which are in their [ ] and also in the [ ] of the entity'. (CIMA Official Terminology, 2005)

Which of the following are the words or phrases omitted from the above definition? Select the words or phrases for EACH of the omissions.

A self-interest

B area of expertise

C best interest

D market

239 Mary is a finance analyst for a small but growing innovative retail company, selling mobile phones via the Internet. The company has only recently listed on the UK stock exchange. At present the company has very few performance indicators. Mary has been tasked with deciding the best measurements to grow the company and ensure survival.

Which THREE of the following indicators would best suit the needs of the company?

A A year on year increase in sales

B An increase in market share

C An increase in the number of hits to their website

D An increase in cash

E The number of customers

F The company's profit

240 D plc is a chain of coffee shops serving fresh ground coffee and pastries. One of the critical success factors (CSFs) is to improve customer satisfaction. Amil, the management accountant of D plc, is looking to measure its performance in a quantifiable way.

Which THREE of the following indicators would best match the CSF identified?

A An increase in positive customer feedback

B An increase in market share

C An increase in the cash flow

D A decrease in the quarterly number of complaints from customers

E The number of customers

F The company's annual profit increasing year on year

241 The public sector is often using the value of money maxim. Within a cancer research charity match the following three elements of the value for money maxim with the appropriate measure.

Element		Measure	
A	Economy	(i)	The number of new treatments available for cancer patients
B	Efficiency	(ii)	The cost savings made due to economies of scale
C	Effectiveness	(iii)	The number of cancer sufferers helped for every pound spent

242 F Ltd is a small privately-owned dentist practice. In recent months, it has experienced severe cash flow problems. However, the owners of the practice feel that the best way forward is to expand the practice into offering more cosmetic dental procedures. The owners are able to finance the practice for a further twelve months with their own funds but after that the practice will have to liquidate if the cosmetic procedures do not generate sufficient income.

Which of the ONE of following investment appraisal techniques would suit the constraints of the dental practice?

- A Net present value appraisal
- B Adjusted present value appraisal
- C A discounted payback calculation
- D Internal rate of return

243 M plc, a large manufacturing company, has just completed a large refurbishment of its head office. Bankole, the management accountant at M plc, has been tasked with investigating why the refurbishment has overspent the budget by 10%. He is considering implementing a post-completion audit.

Which of following are key aims of undertaking a post-completion audit? Select all that apply.

- A To investigate any variances from budget
- B To provide feedback for future projects
- C To avoid repetition of the same mistakes
- D To save money

244 Which TWO of the following are the most important benefits received from conducting a post-completion audit?

- A A post-completion audit encourages greater realism in future forecasting
- B A post-completion audit highlights the reasons for a successful project
- C A post-completion audit can be used to apportion blame
- D A post-completion audit can be used to cut costs in the current project

245 Which of the following statements is/(are) true regarding managerial decisions?

- A The design and use of management control systems affects how an individual makes and implements decisions.
- B Rational managers will always make decisions that are in the best interest of the organisation employing them.

- A Only A is true
- B Only B is true
- C Both A and B are true
- D Neither A nor B is true

SUBJECT P3 : RISK MANAGEMENT

246 'Guide Dogs for the Blind' is a charity whose vision is 'for a society in which blind and partially sighted people enjoy the same freedom of movement as everyone else'. It is wholly financed by private donations.

Which ONE of the following performance indicators would be least appropriate to apply to Guide Dogs for the Blind?

A   Return on capital employed

B   Number of guide dogs trained

C   Increase in donations year on year

D   Reduction in administrative spend per annum

247 S Company has been awarded the contract for the refurbishment of a local hotel. The overall timescale for the project has been agreed at 30 weeks (a very fast completion for this type of project). The timescale is not flexible as the hotel needs to meet this deadline to host a pre-booked wedding. The project has no contingency plan. All other information about the project is vague with the hotel commenting 'we are not the experts, we will let them tell us what we need, after all they should know.'

Which of the following are potential risks to the successful completion of the project? Select all that apply.

A   Unrealistic deadlines means overrun is likely

B   No detailed project plan and specification means misunderstandings between the two parties could occur

C   The hotel might not pay the bill at the end of the refurbishment

D   The wedding might cancel

248 W plc is appraising a new capital project using the Adjusted Present Value method. The finance director has collated the following information regarding the project:

Initial cash outflow	£650 million
Annual cash inflow into perpetuity	£90 million
Cost of equity = 15%	
Financing package:	
10 year loan with interest payable at 9%	£400 million
Tax rate = 35%	

Which ONE of the following is the closest Adjusted Present Value for the project? (To the nearest rounded million.)

A   £280 Million

B   £57 Million

C   £31 Million

D   £2 Million

249 B 8.2%

250 C $6,500,000

Working: Original PV of inflows = $15m + $5m NPV = $20m. NPV of continuing = $20m − ($15m − $4m) − $2.5m = $20m − $11m − $2.5m = $6.5m

251 87.65%

Working: 15-year annuity factor at 10% = 7.606
PV of savings = $1,200,000 × 7.606 = $9,127,200
Certainty equivalent for breakeven = $8,000,000 / $9,127,200 = 87.65%

252 $1.50 million

Working:
- Base case NPV = $600,000 / 0.12 − $4,000,000 = $5,000,000 − $4,000,000 = $1,000,000
- Less issue costs = −$500,000
- PV of tax shield on debt = ($4,000,000 × 8% × 25%) / 0.08 = $80,000 / 0.08 = $1,000,000
- APV = $1,000,000 − $500,000 + $1,000,000 = $1,500,000

253 VPA Co is listed company that is at present 100% equity financed, with a cost of equity of 12%. The directors are reviewing an investment opportunity that would require $2.4 million investment.

The directors feel that the time is now right for VPA to start benefitting from debt finance and plan to fully finance this new investment 100% through this means.

The investment will provide cash inflows, net of tax, of $300,000 for the foreseeable future.

VPA plan to obtain debt from 2 sources, a government subsidy of $1.4 million, subject to interest of 4%, which will be received in perpetuity, and irredeemable bonds at the market rate of 9%.

The issue costs of this debt are not tax deductible and are expected to be 4% of the gross proceeds of issue. The directors intend to issue sufficient debt to cover both the cost of capital expenditure and the costs of issue.

The company's tax rate is 25%.

Calculate the adjusted present value of the investment in $ million. Give your answer in $ million to two decimal places.

$_____ million

---

254 RJS Co makes tyres for a range of vehicles, including motor cars, heavy goods vehicles, motor bikes and bicycles. It is currently financed by a mixture of debt and equity. The FD is currently assessing four new investment opportunities.

Select the best investment appraisal technique for each of the investment scenarios given (Note: you can choose the same technique more than once if you wish)

Projects	Techniques
A – Develop a new range of light weight tyres for racing bikes. Finance by cutting the forthcoming dividend.	Adjusted Present Value
B – Diversify into making cycling helmets. Finance to be raised to maintain the current gearing ratio.	Calculate a NPV using a risk-adjusted WACC
C – Develop a new range of tyres for London busses. RJS can access a subsidized loan as part of the proposal, but intends to use a rights issue as well to keep the financing in line with current levels.	Calculate a NPV using the existing company WACC as a discount rate
D – Developing a range of footwear for cyclists. Finance to be raised via bank loan.	

255 Bohemian Subsidy Co are based in the US, they are currently all equity financed and are looking to take advantage of debt financing for a new venture they are looking into. The discount rate the firm currently uses is 14%.

The machine that they are considering purchasing would cost $10,000,000 and lead to cash inflows of $800,000 for the next 15 years.

They will obtain finance of $6 million from a government subsidised loan at a rate of 3%, with the remainder at the general market rate of 10 %

The Issue costs on the debt finance will be in total $500,000.

The tax rate is 22%

Bohemian Subsidy intends to use an adjusted present value calculation.

What is present value of the financing?.

$_____

256 Q Co is going to invest in a new piece of machinery that will cost $8,000,000. The discount rate of the project is 15% and the PV of the tax shield is $100,000.

What is the IRR? Give your answer as a % to 2 decimal places

_____%

Section 2

ANSWERS TO OBJECTIVE TEST QUESTIONS

IDENTIFICATION, CLASSIFICATION AND EVALUATION OF RISK

1 B

A full definition of risk should allow for both upside and downside aspects and incorporate the concepts of both probability and impact.

2 D

Risk management is the process of reducing the adverse consequences either by reducing the likelihood of an event or its impact.

3 B

Risk appetite is determined by risk attitude and risk capacity.

4 B

The four strategies in TARA are Transfer, Avoid, Reduce, Accept.

5

Pure risks	Speculative risks
The risk that a fire may destroy company assets	The risk that a foreign exchange rate may change
The risk that a customer goes out of business	The risk relating to the level of future profits
The risk that a virus is introduced to a computer application	The risk that a capital investment may not yield the predicted IRR

Note: Pure risks are only 'downside', whereas speculative risks may be 'upside' or 'downside'.

SUBJECT P3 : RISK MANAGEMENT

6 **The six steps in CIMA's risk management cycle are:**

Development of risk response strategy	3
Implement strategy and allocate responsibilities	4
Review and refine process and do it again	6
Identify risk areas	1
Implementation and monitoring of controls	5
Understand and assess scale of risk	2

7

Risk category	Risk
Business risks	Failure of a new product
Economic risks	Inflation rate rises
Environmental risks	Rate of climate change increases
Financial risks	Exchange rate changes

8

Risk category	Risk
Business risks	Raw material prices rise
Economic risks	Disposable income levels fall
Corporate reputation risks	CEO convicted of insider dealing
Political risks	Nationalisation of industry

9

Risk category	Risk
Political risks	Change of Government
Legal risks	Customer sues company for negligence
Regulatory risks	Government increases rate of Corporation Tax
Compliance risks	Company prosecuted for breach of the Data Protection Act

10 A

This is business risk, as it relates to the reputation of product(s), not the Company.

11 B, C, E

12 A, B, C

ANSWERS TO OBJECTIVE TEST QUESTIONS : SECTION 2

13 **A, C**

OKJ's risk analysis should focus on key high-impact, high-uncertainty factors in the organisation's environment.

A falls into this category – it is uncertain whether the government will put in place minimum wage legislation but this could have a significant impact on the company's profits. OKJ definitely needs a contingency plan for this.

B is relatively low impact (thanks to OKJ's insurance) and low uncertainty (OKJ seems confident that it will have to pay the fine), so no further analysis is needed.

C is another factor that is high impact (the cost of platinum rising sharply could cause a fall in profits) and high uncertainty (the movement in metal prices is uncertain, as is the likelihood of a recession). Again, OKJ may wish to consider contingency plans here – such as hedging against platinum price movements.

Finally D appears to be highly uncertain (it is not clear how long the CEO will stay with the company), but low impact (the remaining Board of Directors is capable of minimising disruption to the company), so again this is unlikely to be considered a high risk factor.

14

Term	Definition
risk capacity	'the amount of risk that the organisation is able to bear'
risk attitude	'the overall approach to risk'
risk appetite	'the amount of risk that the organisation is willing to accept in the pursuit of value added'

15 **A, C, D**

The number of directors is irrelevant. Although customers may have expectations regarding risk, this is not a direct determinant of risk appetite.

16 **A**

Although both SWOT and PEST(EL) analysis include external or environmental factors, they are used by managers INSIDE the organisation.

17

    A   Transfer = 2

    B   Accept =1

    C   Reduce = 4

    D   Avoid=3

18 **6 (6MILLION, 6MILLION, $6MILLION, $6MILLION, $6MILLION)**

Once every five years is a probability of 20%. Simply multiply probability and impact to get expected value.

19 **120 (120MILLION, 120MILLION, £120MILLION, £120MILLION, £120MILLION)**

The credit risk exposure is simply the total amount of credit given, not an expected value

SUBJECT P3 : RISK MANAGEMENT

20 **C**

EV = 200 × 0.1 + 250 × 0.4 + 300 × 0.3 + 350 × 0.2 = 280

21 **C**

22 **C, E**

23 **B**

Particularly because it is a small consultancy firm, the death of the CEO would be high impact. However, unless there is a known condition, the probability of sudden death is low.

24 **C**

High staff turnover is common in the industry so probability is high.

Losing one sales person in a large organisation is unlikely to be anything other than low impact.

25 **C**

26 **B**

'Net risk' is calculated by multiplying probability and impact AFTER any action is taken to mitigate the risk.

27 **A, C, D**

A: It is possible that no further planning permission is granted in Country B without the payments.

B: The withdrawal of payments in Country B should have no effect on expansion in Country A since such payments have not been made there.

C: Managers may find it difficult to do their job without the authorisation to make additional payments, become dissatisfied and leave.

D: If expansion into Country B slows or stops overall performance is likely to be affected given that C Company only operates in one other location,

E: This is not a risk of not offering 'extra payments'.

28 **B, C**

A: This is not a risk to Q, rather a government risk.

B: The population of Q may be reluctant to purchase houses in a climate of interest rate rises despite government schemes.

C: If Q has taken out loans to fund expansion (for example to purchase new machinery) costs will increase.

D: The government are unlikely to withdraw schemes since their policy of encouraging people on to the housing ladder will not change.

E: The cost of land will not necessarily increase if interest rates go up, but if Q purchases land by taking out a loan then the costs of servicing the loan will go up.

ANSWERS TO OBJECTIVE TEST QUESTIONS : SECTION 2

29 A, D

A: It seems entirely reasonable to insure equipment but it is likely that internal controls over keeping it safe would also be required.

B: Increasing pay would probably not attract more staff since the scarcity seems to be caused by other factors and staff are already offered generous amounts.

C: It is unlikely that J can accept this. They will need to try and source supplies from alternative suppliers.

D: The 24hr support service is unpopular and is proving expensive with the court case.

30 C

31 A, B, C

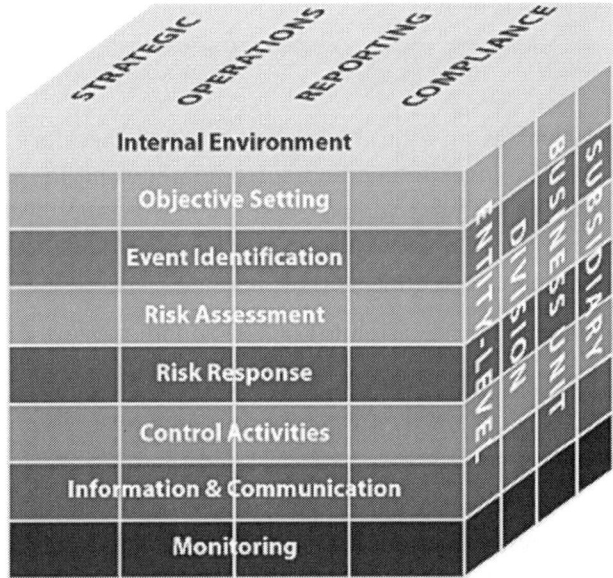

32 A, B, E

COSO considers a WIDE range of risks, and is the responsibility of EVERYONE.

33 All answers are correct

Risk registers record pretty much everything relating to each risk identified

34 A, D, E

The 'missing' elements of the COSO framework are 'Information and communication' and 'monitoring'

35 A

36 B

The Board of Directors are ultimately responsible for a company's system of internal controls.

37 A, C, E

38 B

X has bought a supplier, making it backward vertical integration.

39 A, B, C

These 3 are valid headings for a risk register.

D – is a general term relating to how much risk the business will accept.

E – is a general term relating to the maximum risk the business will accept.

40 A, B, E

C and D are examples of normal business practice.

41 D

MLC have clearly positioned themselves as an ethical company and will therefore attract shareholders who are looking for ethical investments and customers looking for ethically produced goods. If they continue trading with this supplier then their reputation will suffer if the news gets out. By taking strong decisive action and controlling the news story they have demonstrated that they follow their stated ethical principles.

42 ALL OF THEM

43 C

The basic principle here is that of confidentiality. To go outside of the business and professional environment in this manner without first considering the other options presented would not be following recommended process.

A – CIMA's ethics helpline exists to give members advice and is not a breach of confidentiality as it is within the professional arena. B – Reporting the company to the environment agency would comply with relevant legislation, however you would need to sure of your facts before whistle blowing. D – The Audit committee should be all NEDs and therefore a logical place to go, particularly as they are also responsible for the whistle blowing policy.

44 C, D, E

A strong CSR approach may, in fact, increase costs as the organisation has to source its goods more carefully. There is no reason why a strong CSR approach would speed up decision making in the organisation – in fact it is likely to use up management time that could be spent helping to earn the business higher profits. However, CSR often helps to attract both customers and staff, and reduces that chance that governments will be forced to regulate against unethical business behaviour in future.

ANSWERS TO OBJECTIVE TEST QUESTIONS : SECTION 2

45 A, C, D

A: Potential customers can easily switch as the market is competitive.

B: This seems unlikely given that HH sources clothes from many different suppliers.

C: This is a risk since the 'minimum standards' plan will cost money to devise and implement.

D: A recall is more ethical since if successful, it will prevent injury completely.

RESPONSES TO STRATEGIC RISK

46 B, D, F

B – Divisional managers will seek to improve the performance of their divisions but the risk is that the decisions taken may not be in the best interests of the company as a whole.

D – Transfer prices will be needed to correctly account for the expertise and drugs shared between divisions.

F – Performance measures must be fair and motivational to reduce the risk of headhunting.

47 A, D, E

Transfer pricing does not have to be cheap to run, but should ensure that the divisions within Huron work together for the collective benefit of the organisation as a whole.

48 A

$$ROI = \frac{£30,000}{£200,000} = 15\%$$

RI = £30,000 − £24,000 = £6,000.

Since the ROI of the new project exceeds the current after-tax return, it is in the interests of the company to accept it, which the manager of division X will do.

The RI of the project is positive, so will increase the current RI. It will be accepted by the managers.

49 B, E

A – this scheme will be considered unfair and will create a culture of fear, discouraging investment.

B – there is a strong correlation between EVA^{TM} and shareholder value.

C – having two targets could create mixed signals and poor decision making.

D – Managers will still focus on ROI in order to gain the share options, so this will not solve the problem.

E – using NPV will ensure that only projects likely to increase shareholder value are accepted. Using cash flows as a performance metric will motivate managers to achieve the cash flows needed to generate the NPVs calculated.

SUBJECT P3 : RISK MANAGEMENT

50 B

The project is acceptable to the company as a whole, because the RI is positive and the ROI exceeds the target return of 10%.

Based on ROI, the manager of division D will be not be willing to undertake the project, as the project will dilute divisional ROI. However, the positive project RI will increase divisional RI.

51 B

The price must be set high enough for TM to cover its costs, but not so high that RM cannot make a profit.

For TM, an item sold externally has VC of 60% × $24.00 = $14.40.

However, of this, $1.50 will not be incurred on an internal transfer so it is not relevant here, giving an incremental cost on internal transfer = $14.40 – $1.50 = $12.90.

We do not know RM's cost structure, so we leave the price at $12.90. This will ensure that RM is not discouraged from taking an internal transfer when it is profitable to do so.

52 A

Selling frames externally, Division A makes positive contribution of £200 – £120 = £80.

If transferred to B, the Company makes overall contribution of £30 (£300 – (£150 + £120)).

Both are worthwhile but selling frames externally should be prioritised.

Note: The current use of a market price approach leads to Div A being indifferent between selling externally and transferring internally. However, Div B will not want to buy frames internally as it generates a divisional loss on bikes made.

53 A, B, E

The Balance Scorecard (BS) includes a range of measures – including longer-term non-financial measures. It also allows each part of the organisation to create its own indicators.

54 A

The variable cost to company is £70 per unit, whereas the cost of buying in is £76. Since Alpha is not fully occupied, by making no Y its profit will decrease (it loses £88 and saves £70). Company profit must decrease because it pays £76 instead of £70.

55 C

Fully autonomous organisations will have control over revenue, cost and investment levels.

56 A

Managers make decisions based on the targets they are set and how they are evaluated. Not all targets will ensure goal congruence with the overall aims of the main organisation.

ANSWERS TO OBJECTIVE TEST QUESTIONS : **SECTION 2**

57 D

You might want to argue that A, B or even C are commercially preferable to D. However, based on the information provided, there is a high likelihood of the Government of E acting in a way that would result in GS paying more tax then it would under option D.

58 A

Out of the 4 Vs, veracity relates to the risk that with so many different sources there is an increased risk of inaccuracies.

59 D

A lack of consultation, concerns over patient care and a lack of a bonus all mean that surgeons are likely to ignore the new targets.

60 C

Ossification refers to an unwillingness to change the performance measurement mix once it is set up – even if the business needs change.

61 A, D, E

A – predictable demand allows a company to anticipate how much to make, thus reducing the need to hold inventories of finished goods.

B – while this can be helpful, it is less important – it is possible to have JiT with a dedicated process that makes just one product.

C – This is irrelevant.

D – this is very important as suppliers may be asked for extra deliveries at short notice to avoid having to hold inventory of raw materials.

E – the smaller the minimum batch size, the easier it is to tailor production to meet individual customer needs.

62

Category	Cost
Prevention costs	Quality circles
Appraisal costs	Inspection of finished goods
Internal failure costs	Re-working rejected output
External failure costs	Customer returns

SUBJECT P3 : RISK MANAGEMENT

63   B, C, D

A: This measure does not demonstrate the performance of the centre, rather the town in general.

B: This does relate directly to the tourist information centre and so would be a suitable measure to include within the customer perspective.

C: The centre's performance could be measured financially by the amount of revenue it helps to generate for the economy using ticket sales.

D: The centre could demonstrate the number of tourists it assists to show the government how well used it is.

E: Tourists who require more help may go on to spend more money in the town and so a low average time does not necessarily demonstrate strong performance.

64   A, D, E

A: If project managers were assessed on cost as well as successful completion of projects, this would probably lead to fewer external consultants being used.

B: The use of external consultants must be addressed rather than just the cost. This might improve the profit margins slightly but would not help to address the issue of use of external expertise instead of in house staff.

C: Presumably there are occasions where the use of external consultants is justified. The list will need to be retained for such situations. In addition, abolition of the list may lead to poor quality experts being used.

D: If senior management approval was required, project managers would think carefully before requesting external consultant help and unnecessary use of experts would not occur.

E: This would signal whether any particular managers overuse external experts. Such managers could be made aware of the issue.

65   A, B, D

Options A, B and D are not within Fred's control and so if his bonus depends on them he is likely to be demotivated.

Option C, E and F are potentially within Alf's control given the responsibility his employer gives him and so would motivate him to work harder and achieve his bonus.

66   A, B, D

Non-financial benefits include productivity, efficiency and satisfaction.

Expenditure is a financial measure.

ANSWERS TO OBJECTIVE TEST QUESTIONS : SECTION 2

67 A, C

There are several options which will reduce LAP's costs:

A – To avoid using freelancers more full-time staff should be employed. If there is a problem due to salary, then increase the salaries offered. This would still save on costs overall.

B – Overtime would not help if the skills are incorrect in the first place.

C – Full-time staff from other offices ($350) appears to be more expensive than using a freelancer ($300), however, The freelancer is an actual cost (or outflow of cash) whereas the internal recharge is not. Therefore, despite the higher cost of $350 LAP should use internal staff first.

D: Using freelancers 65% of the time = 65 x $300 = $19,500. Using full time staff = 100% x $150 = $15,000. It is cheaper to employ a full-timer overall.

68 A, B, C

Lean management accounting can involve:

- The elimination of variances.
- The reduction of cost centres.
- The reduction in labour utilisation reports.
- Fewer inventory counts due to low inventory levels (JIT production). This is not the case at J as it has to carry high inventory levels to supply the three washing machine manufacturers.

69

Description
These systems allow senior managers to make strategic level decisions
These systems handle large volumes of operational-level data, and support structured decision making.
These systems allow any user with basic training to make semi-structured or unstructured decisions.

Type of system
Executive information
Transaction processing
Expert

70 C, D, E

Managing projects is the role of the Project Managers, while developing new systems will be the job of the project teams.

71 A, C, D

Training and passwords do not mitigate risk in the development process.

72 A, B, D

Pilot changeover cannot be used, as it assumes that any 'lessons learned' in the first changeover can be transferred to all of the other sites. Given each site uses different systems currently it would be difficult to transfer lessons learnt at one site.

SUBJECT P3 : RISK MANAGEMENT

73   **A, D**

Testing reduces the probability of failure, and data backup reduces the impact.

74   **A, B, C, D, E, G**

Applying the balance scorecard:

Customer perspective: C & G

Financial: B & D

Internal: A

Innovation and growth: E

F is not appropriate as it could encourage stores to stock new products regardless of how likely they are to sell.

75   **A, C, E**

76   **B, C, E**

These are the three major reasons for disclosure of confidential information to third parties.

77   **A**

Integrity would be compromised as finance professionals should be straightforward and honest.

78   **B**

Objectivity would be compromised due to the conflict of interest this situation presents.

79   **C**

CPD is needed to maintain professional competence.

80   **D**

Divulging the details requested would breach confidentiality.

81

Refuse to remain associated with the conflict	4
Check the facts	1
Escalate externally	3
Escalate internally	2

82   **A**

John can ultimately benefit financially from his actions so his objectivity may be compromised.

ANSWERS TO OBJECTIVE TEST QUESTIONS : **SECTION 2**

83   **C**

Gemma is being asked to promote a position or opinion to the point that subsequent objectivity may be compromised.

84   **A, B, E**

A: Integrity implies that a person should be straightforward and honest in all business relationships. The management accountant is not being honest because he is helping to produce budgets he knows to be inaccurate.

B: Objectivity: By taking the football tickets in exchange for altering figures the management accountant is allowing bias to override business judgements.

C: The management accountant's skills are not under question and so this principle does not appear to have been breached.

D: The management accountant does not appear to have breached confidentiality. The conversations Stephanie overheard involved Alpha staff and so no information has been leaked.

E: The management accountant has not behaved professionally and in line with CIMA expectations. In addition to using incorrect figures in the budgets he has tried to influence Stephanie to do the same.

85   **A, B, D**

A – TC may feel that by apologising potential customers might feel they were at fault. Legally they had a contract saying that the rooms should be safe and the manager signed it, thus passing the responsibility to the manager. However, morally TC should accept some blame since they didn't check whether the manager had made the rooms safe.

B and C – TC has not explained why it has chosen to award only $350,000 of the $3 million to the parents. The sum seems quite small in comparison, but how much is a child's life worth? The question to many people will be irrelevant. The morally right thing to do would be to give the parents the full $3 million (or more). It is potentially a small sum in comparison to their profits and would go a long way to repairing their reputation. TC's share price has fallen considerably demonstrating the public's feelings for their actions.

D – TC should investigate every room if possible but this would increase TC's costs which would ultimately be passed on to their customers. In each hotel there could be hundreds of rooms and TC may contract with thousands of hotels. It might be more cost efficient to issue strict guidelines on the safety of rooms and ensure they have a tight contract with each hotel. Then they might sample check rooms. The news of the children's deaths should ensure that most hotel owners will check their own hotels since it is their reputation that will be harmed.

E – The publicity that TC has received has not been good and the falling share price demonstrates that not all advertising is good for the company. Sales will potentially fall in future seasons unless TC makes amends.

SUBJECT P3 : RISK MANAGEMENT

86   A, C, D

A – Integrity implies fair dealing and truthfulness. CHB does not meet this criterion as she lied to the council about still being the owner of the business.

B – Objectivity means that CHB should not allow bias or a conflict of interest in business judgements.

C – Confidentiality – The trainee stole the client details and used them to disparage the business. Therefore this ethical principle was not met. CHB should have kept the client details secure.

D – Professional behaviour – CHB has closed the business bank account and changed her telephone number. She does not appear to want to return the $350 rent which she owes. This is theft and not in keeping with the CIMA profession.

E – Professional competence and due care – CHB's professional knowledge and skill is not in question. It is her behaviour that is questionable.

87   D

Answer D is not a benefit of corporate governance since corporate governance is the set of processes and policies by which the company is directed, administered and controlled and will therefore not prevent fraudulent claims by an external party, i.e. contractors.

Answer A is a benefit since good governance will result in a better image with the providers of finance thus making raising finance easier.

Answer B is also a benefit since good governance should result in sustainable wealth creation.

Answer C is a benefit since customers will prefer to purchase a product or service from a company that has a strong reputation for good governance and hence lower levels of risk.

88   D

Directors are placed in control of resources which they do not own and are effectively agents of the shareholders. They should be working in the best interests of the shareholders. However, they may be tempted to act in their own interests, for example by voting themselves huge salaries. The background to the agency problem is the separation of ownership and control – in many large companies the people who own the company (the shareholders) are not the same people as those who control the company (the board of directors).

89   D

External audit is planned by the external auditor. Processing of journals is an operational role and should therefore not be performed by internal audit.

90   B

Chairman and CEO are the two key roles in the organisation and therefore should be held by separate people to dilute power.

91   C, D

92   A, B, C

ANSWERS TO OBJECTIVE TEST QUESTIONS : SECTION 2

93 B, C, D

The remuneration committee should consist of independent NED's only and should not consider NED remuneration. This should be decided by the board as a whole and/or shareholders depending on the specific requirements in the company Articles of Association.

94 B

Non-executive directors are required for a balanced board. A chairman needs to be appointed so the roles of chairman and chief executive can be separate.

95 B

Non-executive directors do not take part in the routine executive management of a company, but must participate at board meetings.

96 C

Whilst the best trigger for the awarding of a bonus would be the director achieving a range of individual performance targets, share options would best align remuneration to shareholder interests as both parties would want the company share price to rise to maximise their individual financial return.

97 B, C, E

A: NED's do not directly set strategies since they have no operational responsibilities. Despite the NED's in the question possibly having the direct experience to enable them to set strategy, this is not their role in governance.

B: Scrutiny of decisions made by the board on behalf of the shareholders is one of the main roles of NED's.

C: Similarly risk monitoring is a role of NED's.

D: External analysis is part of strategy setting and so falls to the executive board to carry out. NED's would be expected to question external analysis but not carry it out in the first instance.

E: The nominations committee is majority NED and would be involved here.

98 A, C

A: The presence of such a senior director would ensure the actions of the chair/CEO were questioned and he or she was held to account. This would make unfettered power less likely and the combined role less risky.

B: This argument suggests the combined role is too great for one individual and so supports a split.

C: This argument suggests that splitting the role will not lead to good governance or guard against corporate failure.

D: If a combined CEO and chairman will be more expensive than a single CEO this is unlikely to be an argument to keep a unified structure.

E: This is a clear argument for splitting the roles.

99   C, D, E

A is incorrect as she is related to the marketing director, she is not independent.

B is not correct because she is not independent, according the corporate governance code the audit committee must be made up entirely of INEDs

C is true, because she is not independent, according the corporate governance code the audit committee must be made up entirely of INEDs

D is true because of her lack of independence, she should not be deciding her father's pay.

E is true, it is unlikely that someone in their first full time job, who has just completed studying is experienced enough to be on the board.

F is incorrect. There are no pre requisites for time served at a company to join the board. Only that to be independent a director cannot have worked at the company within the last five years.

G is not correct. There are no pre requisites for qualifications to join a board. Only that one person on the audit committee has recent and relevant financial experience.

INTERNAL CONTROLS TO MANAGE RISK

100

Category	Example
General	Passwords
Application	Check digits
Software	Licenses
Network	Anti-virus software

101

Category	Example
General	Training
Application	Pre-numbered forms
Software	Licenses
Network	Firewalls

102

Security	Integrity
Locked doors	Batch totals
Passwords	Reconciliation
CCTV	Check digits
Fire alarms	Authorisation of data entry

103   B, D, E

104   B, C, D, E

ANSWERS TO OBJECTIVE TEST QUESTIONS : SECTION 2

105 A

B will not help improve quality itself and therefore does not link to the CSF identified.

C is not specific – how will the company decide if 'quality' is improved by 50%?

D has no measurable target for the amount of training that will be undertaken.

106 C

By definition.

107

	Internal Control	Risk
A	Prepare and reconcile budget to actual spend	1
B	Hedging techniques	4
C	Tight stock control systems	3
D	CCTV cameras in store	2

108 B

2 is an objective of the purchase cycle. 4 is an objective of the payroll cycle.

109 D

1 and 2 are objectives of the purchase cycle.

110 B

1 prevents stock-outs/manufacturing delays. 4 prevents unnecessary goods being ordered.

111 B

2 prevents stock-outs/manufacturing delays. 3 gives assurance about the quality of goods and reliability of supply.

112 B, C

A – Increased training is more likely to increase the rejection rate.

D – Inspections occur before goods get to finished goods inventory.

E – Employing more quality inspectors is more likely to increase the rejection rate.

113 A, B, D

C – Reducing inventory levels may reduce how much thieves can steal but not the number of thefts.

E – Trying to pass the buck to suppliers is unlikely to affect thefts in X's stores.

114 A, B, E

A: If examiners receive more standard training they are likely to behave in a more standardised way, in accordance with the training received.

B: This will reduce the chance of a test centre being accused of being strict or lenient because of its staff.

C and D will not reassure drivers on the test.

E: Should convince learners that they are tested in the same way and to the same standards wherever they take the test.

F: This will not reassure drivers the test is the same, it will just prevent the variations in pass rates seen in the question.

115 B, C

A: Whilst holding more oil would prevent reoccurrence of the late delivery (caused by a stock out), it would increase rather than decrease liquidity risk.

B: This would take the element of judgement away from the inventory manager and ensure that a certain amount of stock was always on hand. Provided this level was set correctly, it should prevent reoccurrence of the problem.

C: If the supplier could reduce lead times it may prevent a stock out but not affect liquidity.

D: This may help with the liquidity problems but not the stock holding costs. In addition, the supplier will be even less inclined to deliver quickly if payment is withheld or delayed.

E: A new supplier of oil would likely bring with it the same issues as G has currently and in addition they are scarce so a new supplier may charge more or be difficult to find.

116 A, D

A: This should reduce the risk of maintenance work being paid for without a record of which flat it relates to. If H has a record of which flat the work relates to, the costs can be recharged.

B: This will help to make sure that invoices are not paid unless work has been done or goods received but will not help H to know which flat the invoice relates to.

C: This may help H to recover more costs than at present but will not reduce the risk of costs not being correctly recharged to flat owners. Some flats with lots of miscellaneous items may not be charged enough and others may be charged too much.

D: This will ensure no invoices are missed and all are recharged.

E: This may ensure all costs are recharged but not correctly to flat owners.

ANSWERS TO OBJECTIVE TEST QUESTIONS : **SECTION 2**

117 A, B, C

A: Q may need to source contractors from outside the local area which is likely to increase costs.

B: Unless Q pays for the insurance which seems unlikely this will be the case.

C: Since local contractors are unlikely to have the accreditation, there will be a shortage and work will back up.

D: There does not appear to be a problem with Q getting the insurance but paying for it seems difficult.

E: This does not appear to be a problem for Q.

118 C

Range checks can help ensure completeness but not security.

119 C

Counterfeiting is a criminal offence and the company may also incur liability for the tort of passing off.

120 A

It would appear that there is no control environment within the company.

121 D

122 B

'Fraud risk is one component of operational risk. Operational risk focuses on the risks associated with errors or events in transaction processing or other business operations. A fraud risk review considers whether these errors or events could be the result of a deliberate act designed to benefit the perpetrator.'

(Taken from the CIMA publication 'Fraud risk management – A guide to good practice')

123 A, B, C

An effective anti-fraud strategy has four main components – prevention, detection, deterrence and response.

(Taken from the CIMA publication 'Fraud risk management – A guide to good practice')

124 A, B, D

CIMA recommends that organisations have:

- a mission statement that refers to quality or, more unusually, to ethics and defines how the organization wants to be regarded externally
- clear policy statements on business ethics and anti-fraud, with explanations about acceptable behaviour in risk prone circumstances
- a route through which suspected fraud can be reported
- a process of reminders about ethical and fraud policies – e.g. annual letter and/or declarations
- an aggressive audit process that concentrates on areas of risk
- management who are seen to be committed through their actions.

(Taken from the CIMA publication 'Fraud risk management – A guide to good practice')

125 A

126 A, B, C

127 B, D, E

128 D

This is a classic example of a Ponzi scheme (or a pyramid scheme).

129 C

Management authorisation will decrease the chances of fraudulent and inaccurate payments being made to non-existent payables.

False billing scams are where companies are sent fraudulent invoices with the hope that some will pay them. Segregation of duties (A) will not prevent such invoices being received. Similarly, neither regular reconciliations between ledgers (B), nor maintaining a trial balance (D) will not identify that the invoices are false. The only way of doing this is to ensure all invoices are authorised as valid before payment.

130 A, C, D

B will not restore shareholder confidence.

E will please shareholders but do nothing about their confidence that similar frauds will not happen again.

F in unfair to the staff concerned who should not be dismissed without following due process and without good reason.

ANSWERS TO OBJECTIVE TEST QUESTIONS : SECTION 2

131 A, B

A: This is definitely a key consideration. The potential cost of reputation risk is high and would far outweigh and cost savings from reduced inspections.

B: Maintenance staff may not do checks as rigorously on the segments and may be less likely to pick up issues.

C: Reporting to management will still take place weekly but be less extensive.

D: Controls should represent value for money (and cost benefit analysis should be carried out), however low cost should not be the overriding priority rather effectiveness.

E: Corrosion checks are internal controls in response to evolving risks and so are relevant to risk assessment.

132 B, C, D

A: Will not prevent theft of finished goods inventory since it relates to raw materials and whether orders are correctly received.

B: Will provide protection from theft by unauthorised access.

C: Will allow R Co to detect fraudulent claims relating to employment history.

D: Will help prevent IT security breaches.

E: Will not help to prevent theft but may assist with rework costs and customer satisfaction.

133 A, C

A: Potential customers unable to enter the car park are likely to park somewhere else leading to a direct loss of revenue.

B: The ticket machines can take payment without issuing a receipt therefore no revenue will be lost.

C: Lack of segregation of duties could lead to potential for fraud.

D, E and F: These are not control weaknesses.

134 A, B, D

135 A, B, D, E

136

Internal Audit	External Audit
Required by shareholders	Required by statute
Reports to Audit Committee or Directors	Reports to Shareholders and Management
Reports on controls	Reports on financial statements

137

Suggestion	Internal Audit Attribute Standard contravened
Jan, as Head of Internal Audit, should report to the Finance Director	Independence
the first project for the new department should be to audit the Treasury Department, which Jan currently manages	Objectivity
It should not be a problem that Jan has no experience of audit and is only part-qualified.	Professional Care
	None contravened

138 D

Finance staff should not be involved with internal audit work. To ensure errors are identified, someone other than the preparer should review the work.

139 Gap 1 – C (competitive), gap 2 – B (internal), gap 3 – A (process)

Competitive benchmarking is likely to help identify risk areas where the firm is performing much worse (or better) than rivals, but it can be difficult to convince a successful rival to share their secrets. As internal benchmarking focuses on other parts of the same organisation, this type of benchmarking often fails to provide insight into performance compared with rivals but can identify under-performing divisions, for example. Process benchmarking can be difficult as there may be few, if any, non-competing businesses that have the same core processes as our organisation. It is therefore often undertaken for non-core activities.

140 A

Ratio analysis is one type of analytical procedure. An analytical procedure requires evaluation of plausible relationships between financial and non-financial information. Inspection, observation and enquiry are different types of auditing techniques.

141 C

1 is incorrect since internal audit would not retain their independence if they reviewed an area for which they had operational responsibility.

3 is incorrect since internal audit would not retain their independence if they implemented controls, their role is to review the controls once implemented.

2 is correct as ISA 610 allows the auditors to obtain direct assistance from internal auditors under supervision of the audit firm.

142 C, D, E

A – family run companies do not necessarily have weaker controls or higher risks.

B – just because the company is a plc, it does not necessarily follow that it is listed.

F – while one would hope the shareholders would want an internal audit department, this reason is not as important as the other factors highlighted.

ANSWERS TO OBJECTIVE TEST QUESTIONS : SECTION 2

143 A, B, C, D

A – compliance audits check the implementation of rules, regulations and procedures. Checking other stores implementation of the discounting policy would be applicable at B retail.

B – a management audit aims to identify existing and potential management weaknesses. Auditor may want to judge whether poor management/staff relations for instance may have led to the breaches in procedure.

C – a systems audit would be appropriate: it would examine the objective of discounting stock, how the procedure works and what the current controls are, other ways to manage discounting etc. The entire process of discounting could be reviewed rather than just whether the current policy is being breached elsewhere. It may be the policy is out of date or the EPOS system can easily be overridden.

D – risk based auditing can be applied in this scenario. It may be the breaches occurred in stores that shared staff or where small stores where it may be more difficult to oversee and supervise staff. Audit may therefore choose to focus on such stores as a priority.

E – environmental auditing is concerned with ensuring environmental safeguarding policies and regulations are being met. This is not applicable in this scenario.

144 D

A systems-based audit is an audit of the internal controls within an organisation. The term can refer to any type of system.

145 A, B, C, D, E

All of the above may apply. Depending on the audit, certain sections may go into more depth.

146 A, B, C

A: This is a key reason why companies outsource internal audit or recruit from outside. Internal candidates can be too close to the organisation to view it objectively.

B: External recruits will not have carried out work in any other role at BGT so this is not a risk.

C: Is another key reason to recruit externally.

D and E are not necessarily the case. Internal recruits may have skills which are more specific and helpful to BGT and internal promotion may be very slow given the concerns over lack of candidates.

SUBJECT P3 : RISK MANAGEMENT

147 A, B

A: The presence of an internal auditor checking the robustness of internal controls can act as deterrent although this is not its primary purpose.

B: Z could make suggestions for improvements but the implementation of such suggestions would be management's responsibility.

C: Internal auditors should not have operational responsibility.

D: Z would only investigate fraud if management asked them to do so. If management were unaware of the fraud then this would not be possible.

E: Again, Z could have only done this at the request of management.

148 B, C, E

A: Internal audit do not carry out any operational work and so would not manage the sales function. Rather, as presented in Option 3 they would oversee the systems changeover and ensure controls are adequate.

B: Investors prefer to see a well monitored company as it reassures them their investment is safe.

C: See comments on Option 1.

D: Best practice dictates that an organisation should review the need for internal audit at regular intervals so not replacing the IA was not a direct contravention.

E: This is a main argument for establishing internal audit.

MANAGING RISKS ASSOCIATED WITH CASH FLOWS

149 A, B, D, E

The only factor given that does not directly affect the demand for or supply of a currency is developments in IT.

150 A

Translation risk relates to the movement in value of assets and liabilities when preparing accounts.

151 C

The Canadian supplier is unaffected as it invoices in its local currency, the Canadian dollar. It will receive the same number of Canadian $ regardless of any movements of the C$ against the £. Eady plc will have to pay more £ to purchase the C$ payable, so will suffer a loss on the weakening of sterling.

152 B

In a period of rising inflation, the prices of commodities tend to go up, while the prices of shares and bonds often tend to go down. Thus, the commodities position will act as an inflation hedge for the stock and bond portfolio.

ANSWERS TO OBJECTIVE TEST QUESTIONS : **SECTION 2**

153 D

In the context of bonds, interest rate risk is the probability of an increase in interest rates causing a bond's price to decrease.

154 C

Political risk is the possibility of an unexpected politically motivated event in a country affecting the outcome of an investment. Political risk analysis will consider the differences between the home and target country, e.g. the stability of government, corruption by officials, different religious beliefs or ethnic tensions.

155 B

The expected value criterion is independent of risk.

156 B

Gross profit	Overheads	Probability
12	Any	0.1
6	4, 3 or 2	0.4 × 0.7 = 0.28
4	3 or 2	0.4 × 0.4 = 0.16
3	2	0.1 × 0.1 = 0.01

Total = 0.55

157 B, C, D

A and E may have an indirect and relatively minor effect.

158 A, B, D, E

A – Assets in the foreign currency can be offset against the liabilities in the same currency

B – Interest costs will be payable in the foreign currency and can be paid from the income in the same currency – i.e. this allows for netting to occur. Netting is a form of internal hedging mitigating transaction risk.

C – False – Simply having a foreign loan does not reduce the downside risk of interest rates increasing.

D – The stability and state of the local banking system may limit local financing.

E – Raising finance locally may also help to maintain the interest of the local government in the success of the business, and there is less risk that the assets will be confiscated.

SUBJECT P3 : RISK MANAGEMENT

EXCHANGE RATE THEORY AND VALUE AT RISK

159 GBP 6,604

Using PPT, the exchange rate in 1 year = 1.5000 × (1.06/1.05) = 1.5143

USD 10,000 then equates to 10,000/1.5143 = GBP 6,604.

160 GBP 1 = EUR 1.2623

Using IRPT, the exchange rate in 1 year = 1.25 – (1.03/1.02) = 1.2623.

161 D

Inflation rates are not relevant to Interest Rate Parity theory (they are relevant to Purchasing Power Parity Theory).

162 7.0%

If the International Fischer effect is true, then the real rate of return in each country should be the same and hence the differences in interest rates can be explained purely due to the differences in inflation.

In Country A the real rate is given by

1 + r = (1 + m)/(1 = i) = 1.113/1.05 = 1.06, so r = 6%

Rearranging this equation for Country B,

1+i = (1 + m)/(1 + r) = 1.1342/1.06 = 1.07, so i = 7%

163 B

Applying interest rate parity:

Invest GBP 1,000 at 5.75% for three months (0.0575/4) = GBP 1,014.375

Convert GBP1,000 to EUR at 1.4415 = EUR 1,441.5

Invest that at 4.75% for three months (0.0475/4) = EUR 1,458.62

Implied forward rate is therefore 1,458.62/1,014.375 = 1.4379

164 USD 707 MILLION

The Z value for a one-tail 95% confidence level is 1.645 (from the Normal Distribution tables).

VaR = standard deviation × Z value, so the

VaR = USD 430 million × 1.645 = 707.35 which rounds to 707.

165 A

Applying interest rate parity:

1.75% × 9/12 = 1.3125

1.40% × 9/12 = 1.05

Spot × (1 + if)/(1 + ih) = 1.3127 × 1.0105/1.013125 = 1.309299

or

Invest GBP 1,000 at 1.75% for nine months (0.0175 × 3/4) = GBP 1,013.125

Convert GBP 1,000 to USD at 1.3127 = USD 1,312.7

Invest that at 1.40% for nine months (0.0140 × 3/4) = USD 1,326.48

Implied forward rate is therefore 1,326.48 /1,013.125 = 1.3093.

166 £115,000

$10,000,000/1.2785 = £7,821,666

Std Dev = 7,821,666 × 0.75% = £58,662.50

Z score for 97.5% = 1.96 (from tables)

VAR = £58,662.50 × 1.96 = £114,978.5

FOREIGN EXCHANGE RATE RISK MANAGEMENT

167 C

Leading with the payment eliminates the foreign currency exposure by removing the liability. Borrowing short-term in Euros to meet the payment obligation in three months' time matches assets and liabilities and provides cover against the exposure. A forward exchange contract is a popular method of hedging against exposure.

168 B

The company will receive Euros through the contracts, so will want a way to sell Euros and receive GBP

A call option gives the holder the right to buy Euros, so is the wrong way round

Forward contracts and MMHs prevent the company from benefiting from any upside potential as they fix the future exchange rate.

169

Internal	External
Leading and lagging	Forward contracts
Matching and netting	Futures
Countertrade	Options

170

Method	Example
Matching	Financing a foreign investment with a foreign currency loan
Netting	Using a foreign currency receipt to offset a foreign currency payment
Pooling	Transferring all bank account balances in one currency into a single account
Countertrade	Exchanging goods or services of similar value

171 A

(1) The investor can buy GBP 500,000 for USD 950,000 compared to USD 975,000 on the spot market.

(2) The investor can sell the GBP 400,000 for SGD 1,160,000 compared to SGD 1,180,000 on the spot market.

The call option should be exercised but the put option should not be exercised.

172 A

First calculate the number of contracts using the STRIKE price so

USD 5m/1.6 = GBP 3,125,000 then at a contract size of GBP 25,000.

SGB will take an option on GBP 3,125,000/25000 = 125 contracts.

The premium is USD 1,000 per contract so USD 125,000 as a premium must be paid to the exchange when the contract is taken out so this transaction will be done at the current spot of 1.5500.

125,000/1.5500 = GBP 80,645.

173   32,531

X will be looking to buy USD so the starting point is the spot rate of 1.5400

You need to subtract a premium so the forward rate = 1.5400 − 0.0030 = 1.5370

GBP cost = 50,000/1.5370 = 32,531.

174   849,248

The hedge requires X to borrow in GBP, translate to EUR and deposit EUR. The deposit (plus interest) can then be used to pay the supplier.

A payment of EUR 1million in 6 months will require a EUR deposit (earning 1% interest) now of 1,000,000/1.01 = EUR 990,099.

Using a spot rate of 1.195 this requires X to borrow 990,099/1.195 = GBP 828,535. This is borrowed at an interest rate of 2.5%.

Repayment of the loan will cost X 828,535 × 1.025 = GBP 849,248.

ANSWERS TO OBJECTIVE TEST QUESTIONS : SECTION 2

175   USD 41,835,000

DWTV will need to BUY GBP to pay their UK supplier and would naturally wish to pay the lowest price per GBP which would be 1.6700, so they exercise the option. (At 1.6700 GBP 25m would cost USD 41,750,000 whereas at 1.6850 it will cost USD 42,125,000)

However they must also have paid the premium of USD 85,000 taking the total cost to 41,750,000 + 85,000 = 41,835,000

176   LOSS = £5,625

Pogs are committed to buy gilts with a face value of £1,000,000 (£500 × 2,000)

The value position fell from 119 8/16 to 118 15/16

Pogs bought, so they are making a loss.

Opening position: £1,000,000 × 119 8/16/100 = 1,195,000

Closing position: £1,000,000 × 118 15/16/100 = 1,189,375

The loss = £5,625

177   D

As they are due to receive EUR, they will be selling & the bank buying, therefore the higher rate is used: 1.7027

There is a discount of 2.5 cents, which will be added to the spot rate as EUR will be less valuable in the future.

1.7027 + 0.0250 = 1.7277

700,000/1.7277 = 405,162.93

178   GBP 798,044.08

If APS exercise the option they would receive EUR 1,200,000/1.4405 = GBP 833,044.08

If APS sell EUR on the spot market, they would receive EUR 1,200,000/1.4640 = 819,672.13

The option is therefore 'in the money' and so APS will exercise the option.

They have paid a premium of GBP 35,000, so the net receipt is:

833,044.08 – 35,000 = GBP 798,044.08

179 $6,426,000

6 months		Now
Pay £6,000,000	Create £ asset today ->	**Deposit** in £ enough to be pay off the liability in 6 months. 6,000,000/1.025 = £5,853,658.54
		Translate into USD at the spot rate £5,853,658.54/0.9610 = 6,091,215.96
$6,426,232.84	Incur interest for 6 months at 11% $6,091,215.96 × 1.055 <-	**Borrow** $6,091,215.96 in the US

109

SUBJECT P3 : RISK MANAGEMENT

180 D

We need the contract size and the transaction in GBP, use the strike price

$4,000,000/1.4500 = 2,758,621 (if you chose C you used the spot rate)

Now we work out the number of contracts:

2,758,621/25,000 = 110.34484

So that's 111 contracts (if you chose B you rounded down)

At $2,500 per contract this would cost $277,500, but we need the cost in GBP (if you chose A you stopped too early)

$277,500/1.2750 = **£217,647**

We use the spot as the transaction is taking place today (if you chose E you used the strike price).

181 A, C and E

Cut is committed to deliver gilts with a face value of £500,000 (£500 × 1,000)

The value of the position fell from 124 53/64 to 121 8/64

Cut sold, so they are making a profit.

Opening position: £500,000 × 124 53/64/100 = £624,141

Closing position: £500,000 × 121 8/64/100 = £605,625

Profit = £18,516

182 C

(1) Xavier can buy GBP 800,000 for EUR 960,000 compared to EUR 920,000 on the spot market.

(2) Xavier can sell the GBP 1,000,000 for USD 1,300,000 compared to USD 1,250,000 on the spot market.

The call option should not be exercised, but the put option should be exercised.

INTEREST RATE RISK MANAGEMENT

183

Instrument	Description
Forward Rate Agreement (FRA)	An over the counter instrument, with a fixed rate
Interest Rate Guarantee (IRG)	An over the counter instrument, hedging only downside risk
Future	A traded instrument, with a fixed rate
Option	A traded instrument, hedging only downside risk

184 6.20%

The reference rate of 6.00% is higher than the FRA rate of 5.70% (banks sell high, remember) so the FRA will be settled by a payment to X of 0.30%.

The actual rate paid on the loan is 6.50% (base plus 0.50%), and deducting the FRA receipt of 0.30% gives an effective rate of 6.20%.

ANSWERS TO OBJECTIVE TEST QUESTIONS : SECTION 2

185 A

An interest-rate cap will pay its owner the maximum of zero or the market rate minus the cap rate, times the notional principal. An interest rate cap is a bundle of interest rate calls with successive expiry dates, whereas an interest rate floor is a bundle of interest rate puts.

186 D

DD Co pays LIBOR + 1.5% at the moment and the bank has offered a swap at the rate of 5% for LIBOR (i.e. DD Co will pay 5% to the bank in exchange for LIBOR).

Hence the net rate is (LIBOR + 1.5%) + 5% − LIBOR = 6.5%

187 D

There is a bigger difference in the variable rates so to take advantage of this, B will borrow variable and A then has to borrow at a fixed rate.

Use L% to get B on fixed and A on variable. Then 3.5% is the balancing figure to split the saving on an equal basis.

It would work out like:

	Co A	Co B
Paid to bank	(7%)	(L+2%)
A pays B	(L)	L
B pays A	3.5%	(3.5%)
Net effect	(L + 3.5%)	(5.5%)

188 B, C

A   Selling FRAs would be appropriate if Grudem was looking to *deposit* funds.

B   Options to sell STIRs will protect against interest rate rises but allow Grudem to benefit from any falls.

C   Buying an interest rate cap will protect against interest rate rises.

D   Buying bond futures would be appropriate if Grudem was looking to *deposit* funds.

189

Situation	Calculations
Company has a loan and a cap where the strike rate is higher than the market rate	Market rate + premium costs
Company has a deposit and a floor where the strike rate is higher than the market rate	Strike rate − premium costs
Company has a loan and a cap where the strike rate is less than the market rate	Strike rate + premium costs
Company has a deposit and a floor where the strike rate is less than the market rate	Market rate − premium costs

Where the company has a loan we would have to add the premium costs to the loan as in the case of A and C and deduct in the case of a deposit (B and D).

All that then needs to be resolved is whether we exercise the option or allow it to lapse. If we exercise we would use the strike rate if we lapse we would use the market rate.

To determine whether to exercise or lapse we have to consider whether we are looking at a loan or a deposit.

SUBJECT P3 : RISK MANAGEMENT

If it is a loan we would want to minimise loan costs so we would pick the lowest rate: in the case of A this would be market rate, which means lapsing the option and using the market rate. Whereas in the case of C the reverse is true we would exercise and use the strike rate.

If it is a deposit we would want to maximise our interest rate returns and therefore if the strike rate is higher than the market as in the case of B, we would exercise the option and use the strike rate (but we deduct the premium costs to get the net benefit).

190

Required position	Combination of options
A 'cap' on the interest rate on a loan	Buy a Call on a FRA
A 'floor' on the interest rate on a deposit	Buy a Put on a FRA
A 'collar' to protect the interest cost of a loan	Buy a Call on a FRA and sell a put on a FRA
A 'collar' to protect the interest on a deposit	Buy a Put on a FRA and sell a call on a FRA

Caps place a ceiling on the interest rate costs of a loan, buying the right to buy a FRA will mean that if rates rise the company can buy the FRA and get the counterparty to compensate them, thus reducing the effective loan cost. In a similar way buying a put on a FRA will mean that if rates fall too much they will be able to sell A FRA and benefit from the fall in rates. In the case of the two collars, you will notice that you start the same way as before. In the case of a loan you buy a call paying premium but you simultaneously sell a put thus receiving premium, this reduces the overall premium costs. For a deposit you buy a put in order to protect its value but simultaneously sell a call to reduce premium costs.

191 A

Interest rate options are the right to buy or sell interest rate futures. The option will only be exercised in order to make a profit on the futures which will help to mitigate any losses on a loan due to a rise in interest rates. Interest rate options do not give entitlement to a loan. The loan is taken out independently of the options. An interest rate option does not give the right to an interest rate. It effectively reduces loan costs when interest rates rise adversely by providing a profit on the futures that have been bought or sold.

192 C, D

An interest rate floor would be used for a deposit and not a loan thus the second statement is not true. To achieve this, the company would need to buy a put option on a FRA not a call. Again the last statement will be ruled out as false as floors are used for deposits not for loans. A floor is a means of protecting the interest rate on a variable rate deposit so is particularly useful when interest rates are thought likely to fall. As the premium costs have to be paid this will effectively reduce the interest received on the loan.

193 A, C, D, E

All of these are inputs into the Black Scholes model with the exception of the tax rate.

194 C

Investors 'close out' their positions and therefore either win or lose cash.

ANSWERS TO OBJECTIVE TEST QUESTIONS : SECTION 2

195 B

OTC derivative contracts (securities) are customized and have poor liquidity.

The contract is with a specific counterparty and there is default risk since there is no clearing house to guarantee performance.

196 A

The existence of derivatives markets does not affect the level of interest rates. The other statements are true.

197 C, E, F

Options do not provide complete certainty as to the amount paid or received as they may or may not be exercised but they do ensure that the cash flows associated with financing the transaction are known in advance as the premium has to be paid up front regardless of what happens. This is in contrast with futures where there is some variation in cash flows associated with the transaction as variation margin may have to be paid. They are far from being simple, cheap or easy to understand but they are very useful for hedging uncertain transactions as they are a right and not an obligation to do something. In other words they need not be exercised.

198 B

As the loan starts in 6 months, they will use the 6 V 15 option at 3.45 – 3.7.

As they are taking out a loan the bank will be charging them the higher rate, 3.7%.

As it's L + 0.55 and the FRA is at 3.7%, the company will pay 3.7 + 0.55 = 4.25%.

199 B, E

Is the swap feasible?

Want – 7% + LIBOR + 3.3% = LIBOR + 10.3%

Opposite – 8% + LIBOR + 2% = LIBOR + 10%

A swap would only work if M wanted fixed and D wanted variable, that is the case here, so a swap will happen.

The overall benefit is 0.3%.

M will receive (0.3 × 0.60 =) 0.18%

D will receive (0.3 × 0.40 =) 0.12%

Therefore M will end up 0.18% better off than borrowing from the bank so pays

7% - 0.18% = 6.82%

D will end up 0.12% better off than borrowing from the bank so pays

LIBOR + 3.3% - 0.12% = LIBOR + 3.18%.

SUBJECT P3 : RISK MANAGEMENT

200 B, E, F

The original (put) option provides a ceiling at 5.5%, the second (call) option then creates the floor at (100 – 95.05 =) 4.95%.

The premium would be:	%
Pays premium on put	(0.85)
Receives premium on call	0.34
Net premium	(0.51)

201 A, D, F

UB50 have variable and want fixed:

Pay lender	(L + 4.5)
Receive from bank	L
Pay bank	(7.5)
Net interest rate	(12)

Bid = 7.4% (the amount the bank is willing to pay)

Ask = 7.5% (the amount the bank is willing to receive).

202 B

An interest rate floor guarantees that the interest rate the owner of the floor receives on a deposit does not drop below a certain level, so if the interest does drop below they receive a top up payment to keep them at the floor level.

An interest rate floor is a bundle of interest rate puts with successive expiry dates, whereas an interest rate cap is a bundle of interest rate calls.

203 A, B, E, F

- A Selling FRAs protects Tither from interest rate falls by fixing the rate they will receive.
- B Tither matches its assets and liabilities to have a common interest rate (i.e. loan and investment both have floating rates).
- C Options to sell STIRs will protect against interest rate rises but allow Tither to benefit from any falls, so would be appropriate for a loan.
- D Buying an interest rate cap will protect against interest rate rises, as Tither are depositing they would want interest rates to rise, so this is inappropriate.
- E Buying bond futures is appropriate as Tither is looking to deposit funds.
- F Tither will try to maintain a certain balance between its fixed rate and floating rate borrowing. The portfolio of fixed and floating rate debts thus provide a natural hedge against changes in interest rates. There will be less exposure to the adverse effects of each but there will also be less exposure to any favourable movements in the interest rate.

MANAGING RISKS ASSOCIATED WITH CAPITAL INVESTMENT DECISIONS

204 C

205 D

206 D

The risk free rate is used, as risk has already been adjusted for by using certainty equivalent cash flows.

207

Projects	Techniques
A – Develop a new range of light weight crossbows. Finance by cutting the forthcoming dividend	Calculate a NPV using the existing company WACC as a discount rate
B – Diversify into making luxury yachts. Finance to be raised to maintain the current gearing ratio	Calculate a NPV using a risk-adjusted WACC
C – Develop a new range of weapons for the police force of Country P. SCW can access a subsidized loan as part of the proposal	Adjusted Present Value
D – Building a new range of fly fishing reels. Finance to be raised via a rights issue.	Calculate a NPV using the existing company WACC as a discount rate

Note:

- The company WACC can only be used if both business risk and gearing remain unchanged by the project.
- A risk adjusted WACC is used when the project has different business risk than the company but the gearing will remain unchanged.
- APV must be used when there is a change in gearing.

208 B

The IRR (C) and the cost of the initial investment (A) are independent of the risk of the project. The higher the risk of the project, then the higher (not lower – D) the required rate of return.

209 A

The use of general purpose equipment makes it easier and less expensive to abandon using the factory if economic circumstances change.

210 252,632

(ACS × 0.95)/0.08 = $3,000,000

ACS = ($3,000,000 × 0.08)/0.95 = $252,632

SUBJECT P3 : RISK MANAGEMENT

211 A

Creditors bear the responsibility for bankruptcy in that they will not receive the principal back from their investment. If the project is a great success, creditors' returns will not increase, they will only receive the money loaned plus interest. On the other hand, shareholders could see the value of their shares rise many times over, while the reputation of the managers (and their bonuses) is likely to rapidly increase.

212 C

The project involves a change in the gearing level, so the APV method must be used.

A is wrong as the WACC will change as a result of the project.

B is wrong as the company has debt as well as equity finance.

D is not appropriate as the shareholders are not well-diversified.

213 D

The project involves a change in the gearing level, so the APV method must be used. However, this option is not given, so we must consider which calculations are needed as part of APV. The base case NPV would involve calculating an ungeared cost of equity (not the company's existing Ke) using CAPM, so D is the correct answer.

214 B, D

The WACC calculation should incorporate all long term methods of finance.

215 D

The shareholders are likely to be well-diversified so unaffected by changes in unsystematic risk (A and B). Systematic risk may change as the beta factors in the different markets are unlikely to be the same (C).

216 B

It is a collective responsibility of the board of directors, although it is often delegated to the finance director to deal with on their behalf.

217 A, C, D

218 A (III), B (I), C (IV), D (II)

Beta Value	Required rate of return
Beta value less than one	The shares have less systematic risk than the market average, therefore the investor will require a lower than average return
Beta value greater than one	The shares have more systematic risk than the market average, therefore the investor will require a higher than average return
Beta value equal to zero	The shares have no systematic risk, therefore the investor will require a risk free rate of return
Beta value equal to one	The shares have the same systematic risk as the market average, therefore the investor will require an average return

ANSWERS TO OBJECTIVE TEST QUESTIONS : SECTION 2

219 A

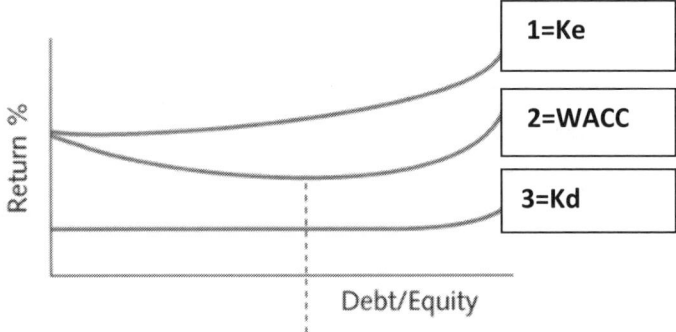

220 D

Outcome (x)	Probability p(x)	x.p(x)
(£5,000)	0.20	(£1,000)
£1,000	0.30	£300
£7,000	0.40	£2,800
£12,000	0.10	£1,200
	E(x)	£3,300

221 C

1 = Unsystematic risk, 2 = Total risk, 3 = Systematic risk

222 B

Having half the risk of the market average implies a beta of 0.5

223 D

Advertising has the highest systematic risk as indicated by having the highest beta.

224 A, B

Scenario I: NPV (£'000) = −100 + 55/1.12 + 70/1.12^2 = + 4.91

Scenario II: NPV (£'000) = −100 + 55/1.15 + 70/1.15^2 = + 0.76

Scenario III: NPV (£'000) = −100 + 55/1.19 + 70/1.19^2 = − 4.35

225 C

Units sold	Revenue	Probability	Expected Return
80	$800	0.15	$120
100	$1,000	0.50	$500
120	$1,200	0.35	$420
		1.00	$1,040

117

226 B

Product X NPV £	Probability (%)	Expected value
3,000	10	300
3,500	20	700
4,000	40	1,600
4,500	20	900
5,000	10	500

Total X = 4,000

Product Y NPV £	Probability (%)	Expected value
2,000	5	100
3,000	10	300
4,000	40	1,600
5,000	25	1,250
6,000	20	1,200

Total Y = 4,450

227 C

If 70 salads will be required on 75 days of a 250-day year, the probability that demand:

P(Demand of 70) = 75 days ÷ 250 days

P(Demand of 70) = 0.3

228 D

(5/40 × 6%) + (5/40 × 10%) + (30/40 × 15%) = 13.25%

229 A

230 C

231 B

232 B

233 A, C

Note: interest payments are only relevant if, say, a subsidised loan is used, in which case it is the SAVING in interest rates, not the total figure that is relevant.

234 B

ANSWERS TO OBJECTIVE TEST QUESTIONS : SECTION 2

235 A (II), B (I), C (IV), D (III)

Stakeholder			Goals	
A	Equity investors		(ii)	The strategy will need to result in a higher return
B	Customers		(i)	The value for money of products must at least remain, if not improve
C	Employees		(iv)	Long term security of X plc
D	UK suppliers		(iii)	The partnership will end

236 A, B, C, D

The reduction in quality is likely to result in a long term fall in reputation, market share, customer satisfaction and shareholder value.

237 B, D

Even though against his own personal interests, Mr Big should take steps consistent with maximising shareholder value.

238 A, C

A definition of goal congruence within a control system is 'the state which leads individuals or groups to take actions which are in their self-interest and also in the best interest of the entity' (CIMA Official Terminology, 2005).

239 A, B, D

240 A, B, D

241 A (II), B (III), C (I)

Element		Measure	
A	Economy	(ii)	The cost savings made due to economies of scale
B	Efficiency	(iii)	The number of cancer sufferers helped for every pound spent
C	Effectiveness	(i)	The number of new treatments available for cancer patients

242 C

The emphasis on liquidity makes payback a more suitable technique here

243 A, B, C

244 A, B

245 A

SUBJECT P3 : RISK MANAGEMENT

246 A

247 A, B

248 C

Base case NPV = –650 + (90/0.15) = –50

PV of financing side effects = (400 × 0.09 × 0.35) × 6.418 = 80.87

APV = –50 + 80.87 = + 30.87

249 A

The IRR is the discount rate where the NPV falls to zero.

It is a really a sensitivity calculation, the questions we need to ask ourselves are as follows:

(1) How much would the NPV need to change by? 450,000

(2) What is this as a % of the investment? 450,000/18,000,000 × 100 = 2.50%

So if the discount rate reduced by 2.5% the NPV would fall to zero.

IRR = 8% × 97.5% = 7.8%

250 C

The $4million that has already been spent is now sunk, there is an additional (and immediate) cost of $2.5 million.

NPV = $5 million add back the sunk cost as it is no longer relevant $4 million then take off the new cost of $2.5 million = 5 + 4 – 2.5 = $6.5 million

251 87.65%

The breakeven point of the project is when the NPV = 0.

The NPV will equal zero when the PV of the inflows is equal to the PV of the outflows.

8,000,000 = 1,200,000 × 7.606 × CE

8,000,000/(1,200,000 × 7.606) = CE

CE = 87.65%

252 A

Base case:

Year	Cashflow $	DF @ 12%	PV $
0	-4,000,000	1	-4,000,000
1 - ∞	600,000	1/0.12	5,000,000
			1,000,000

Financing:

	$		$
Interest	4,500,000	0.08	360,000
Tax saving/year	360,000	0.25	90,000
Tax saving in perpetuity	90,000	1/0.08	1,125,000
Issue costs			-500,000

APV

1,000,000 + 1,125,000 -500,000 = 1,625,000

Answer = 1.63

253 1.01

Base case

Year	Cashflow $	DF @ 12%	PV $
0	-2,400,000	1	-2,400,000
1 - ∞	300,000	1/0.12	2,500,000
			100,000

Financing

Actual finance to be issued: 2,400,000/0.96 = 2,500,000

Tax relief on debt interest

	$		$
Interest – market rate debt	1,100,000	0.09	99,000
- Government subsidy	1,400,000	0.04	56,000
		Total annual interest	**155,000**
Tax saving/year	155,000	0.25	38,750
Tax saving in perpetuity	38,750	1/0.09	**430,555.56**

Value of the subsidy

	$		$
PV of Interest saved	1,400,000	(0.09-0.04) × 1/0.09	777,777.78
Less PV of tax relief lost	70,000	0.25 × 1/0.09	-194,444.44
1,400,000 × (0.09 – 0.04) = 70,000			**583,333.34**

Issue costs			100,000

APV

100,000 + 430,555.56 + 583,333.34 -100,000 = 1,013,888.90. Answer = 1.01

254

Projects	Techniques
A – Develop a new range of light weight tyres for racing bikes. Finance by cutting the forthcoming dividend.	Adjusted Present Value
B – Diversify into making cycling helmets. Finance to be raised to maintain the current gearing ratio.	Calculate a NPV using a risk-adjusted WACC
C – Develop a new range of tyres for London busses. RJS can access a subsidized loan as part of the proposal, but intends to use a rights issue as well to keep the financing in line with current levels.	Calculate a NPV using the existing company WACC as a discount rate
D – Developing a range of footwear for cyclists. Finance to be raised via bank loan.	Adjusted Present Value

Note:

- The company WACC can only be used if both business risk and gearing remain unchanged by the project.

- A risk adjusted WACC is used when the project has different business risk than the company but the gearing will remain unchanged.

- APV must be used when there is a change in gearing.

255   2,962,251.20

Tax relief on debt interest

	$		$
Interest – market rate debt	6,000,000	0.03	180,000
- Government subsidy	4,000,000	0.10	400,000
		Total annual interest	580,000
Tax saving/year	580,000	0.22	127,600
PV of tax saving	127,600	7.606	**970,525.60**

Value of the subsidy

	$		$
PV of Interest saved	6,000,000	(0.1-0.03) × 7.606	3,194,520
Less PV of tax relief lost	6,000,000 × 0.07	0.22 × 7.606	-702,794.40
			2,491,725.60

Issue costs			500,000

PV of financing = 970,525.60 + 2,491,725.60 – 500,000 = 2,962,251.20

ANSWERS TO OBJECTIVE TEST QUESTIONS : SECTION 2

256   14.81

The IRR is the discount rate where the NPV falls to zero.

It is a really a sensitivity calculation, the questions we need to ask ourselves are as follows:

(1)   How much would the NPV need to change by?   100,000

(2)   What is this as a % of the investment?   100,000/8,000,000 × 100 = 1.25%

So if the discount rate reduced by 1.25% the NPV would fall to zero.

IRR = 15% × 98.75% = 14.8125

Answer: 14.81.